Elephant Rock

Craig S Buehner

Cover design by Rob Hinckley

Printed in the United States of America

TO MY WIFE DONNETTE,
I CAN'T IMAGINE LIFE'S JOURNEY WITHOUT
YOU.

CHAPTER 1

High Expectations

It was a beautiful early summer morning, a perfect start to a day I'd been working toward for months. Even the stalled traffic couldn't dampen my spirits. I smiled as we inched slowly toward the freeway exit to my downtown office, cracking my window to inhale the smell of early summer. Excitement surged through my veins. The Partition Project I had been spearheading for the last few months had been an unqualified success, bringing millions of dollars to the company. The Board of Directors met yesterday to appoint a new executive to serve on the team. Who else could it be? I was a shoo-in. The Partition Project was my idea from start to finish. At twenty-five I could become the youngest executive in the company's history. I parked in the garage and headed to the elevator. As I exited at the fifteenth floor, the receptionist greeted me cheerfully.

"Good morning Chance," she said, smiling and handing me a note.

"Good morning Liz. What's this?"

"Mr. Gilmer asked me to give it to you the moment you walked through the door." I smiled and my heart raced as I turned the paper over:

Chance Backerton

Executive boardroom, 8:30 sharp! Be there.

Gilmer

I stifled the urge to leap into the air, and walked calmly to my office. I really had it all — a gorgeous wife, two beautiful little girls, a brand new home, a corner office, and the most successful project this company had ever known. Now there was only one piece missing — the final patent approval for the Partition Project. My dad used to say, "You can accomplish anything if you just set your mind to it." This morning I was glad I'd believed in his advice.

I swiveled in my chair and looked out the window. What a beautiful morning! The weather had changed abruptly from my drive into the office, and now the skies held dark clouds that promised pouring rain. I didn't care. I kicked off my shoes and put my feet up on my desk. I leaned forward and turned on my computer, placing the keyboard in my lap.

A quick glance at the clock told me I had about thirty minutes before I had to meet Mr. Gilmer. Just enough time to answer a few emails, I thought. As I paged through my inbox an email caught my eye. The heading read, Partition Project receives final patent approval. "Yes!" I shouted. From my first day on the job, this project had been my only focus. I had developed a new, more efficient way to compartmentalize multiple hard drives within a network, which greatly increased their speed; basically, it revolutionized the entire process. The technology was cutting-edge, and my work was the basis of my company's application for a patent.

Could this day get any better? My promotion to executive was in the bag. There's no way they could pass me by, even though I was much younger than the others in the office. Most had been with the company for many years, including my project manager, Bob Sparks. As much as I wanted this promotion, I would understand if the board promoted Bob ahead of me. He'd been with the company 30 years, after all. If push came to shove, I could wait another year.

Bob didn't seem to want to work too hard anymore, though. He always seemed content to do just enough to get a check, never working a minute longer than necessary. When five o'clock hit, he was out the door. Not me. I was at the office late every night, doing what it took to succeed. I never went home until the job was done. It didn't make my wife Kelsea too happy, but hey, work is work. After a while, she seemed to get used to me never being home. But today all those long hours would finally pay off.

Now it was time to collect my reward. I slipped my shoes back on and picked up my suit coat, straightening my tie as I walked to the elevator. As I pressed the button for the fourteenth floor I couldn't help wondering if they would move my office so I could be closer to the other executives. Last year when Mike Langston was voted in as an executive, he was moved.

As the doors opened, I nearly ran into Mike. Speak of the devil.

"Hey, Mike!" I said enthusiastically. He looked at me, shook his head, and just kept walking.

The stunned look on his face took some of the wind out of my sails. He wasn't happy, and I figured something must be wrong. My stomach churned. I hope they didn't demote him to make room for me! He has five kids and is much older than I am. But, I've brought so much more value to the company, I thought as I walked through the large glass doors leading into the executive floor.

The executive assistant greeted me with a smile. "They're waiting for you in the conference room Mr. Backerton," she said warmly. She's in an extra-good mood today, I thought.

I made my way to the conference room and slowly opened the door. "Mr. Backerton, please have a seat," said Mr. Gilmer.

I didn't sit down immediately. I glanced around the room suddenly conscious that every member of the board was seated around the table.

They smiled at me, with the exception of my direct boss, Mr. Gilmer. He never smiles when the board meets. Mr. Gilmer sat at the head of the table accompanied by Ms. Morison, and Mr. Barnes. I felt butterflies beginning to swarm in my stomach.

"Have a seat, Chance. We'll get right to it," Mr. Gilmer said abruptly.

Mr. Gilmer likes to get right to the point. He's a corporate machine. At least I always knew exactly where I stood with him. I sat down in the only unoccupied chair, sinking into the soft leather. I had a feeling the outcome of this meeting was going to change my life.

My focus was on Mr. Gilmer, but to my surprise Ms. Morison was the first to speak. "Chance, I'm afraid we have bad news," she began.

My heart sank. Bad news? How could there be bad news? I'm here for good news. They must have fired Bob Sparks and they weren't quite sure how I would take it.

"The company has suffered a few setbacks," Ms. Morison continued. "First the mainframe debacle and then the chipset union strike have cost the company millions. Our stock has tumbled and our shareholders want blood."

"I'm aware of both situations, but I'm not sure how that affects me," I interrupted quickly. "The Partition Project has been a huge success. In fact, the final patent cleared this morning. I thought that was the reason why I was —"

"Yes, Mr. Backerton, I am very aware of your success with the Partition Project, and we thank you for that." Ms. Morison didn't even allow me to finish my statement. She sat back and took a deep breath. "The board met yesterday and had to make some very hard decisions."

"Hard decisions. Like pay cuts?" I choked.

"Among other things. Mr. Backerton this is hard enough as it is. We will allow you time to ask questions, but please let me finish," Ms. Morison said. I sat in stunned silence. The butterflies I felt just moments ago had died, and now were replaced by a heavy, queasy feeling emanating from the pit of my stomach. As beads of sweat began to build on my forehead, I put a finger in my collar and pulled it away from my neck. What a difference ten minutes can make.

"We've been instructed to terminate forty percent of our most highly paid employees. The question as to who to terminate has been very difficult. In an effort to keep things fair, you will no longer be working for the company," she said.

The room fell dead silent. The only sound I could hear was the mechanical tick-tick-tick as the clock marked the passing seconds, the countdown timer of the bomb within me that felt ready to explode. I struggled to suppress the imminent explosion, somehow managing to remain calm.

"In an effort to keep things fair?" I gasped. "I don't understand how you could choose me? The Partition Project is mine! I thought of the idea and found a market for it. Why me?"

"It wasn't because of a lack of talent or your abilities. The decision was based mostly on your age. Many of our employees have been working for the company most of their lives. You're young and adaptable. You'll land on your feet," Ms. Morison answered.

"So I'm being discriminated against because of my age?" I demanded?

"Call it what you will, but trust me when I say we're on solid legal ground. You're not the only one. The cuts extend across all classes of people within the company."

"So, basically I'm screwed," I spat back.

"Mr. Backerton, you're young and bright. You'll be fine."

"Yeah, you're right; I'll be fine," I answered sarcastically. I paused for a moment as the others exchanged brief, relieved glances. Those didn't last long.

"I'll take the Partition Project with me. It's my idea. I'll do it on my own. I'm certain investors would be more than willing to put money into a proven system," I answered brashly, sitting up straight and squaring my shoulders.

Mr. Gilmer reached for his phone. "We expected that you might threaten that," he said, glancing at me as he dialed. "Will you please send in Mr. Rooker?" he said.

The door opened and the company attorney, Mr. Rooker, entered. He wore a stone cold expression, placing his briefcase on the table and leaning over to shake my hand. He sat down next to me, opened his briefcase, and retrieved a thick document. He flipped to the last page and placed it in front of me.

"Mr. Backerton, is this your signature?" He pointed to the bottom of the page. I recognized the document as the contract I had signed two years ago.

"Yes it is," I answered.

Rooker produced a second document, placed it in front of me and asked the same question.

"Yes. That is also my signature, but I'm not sure what this is," I said.

"Allow me to enlighten you," Mr. Rooker said smugly. "This document is a non-compete, which states for the period of two years beyond your termination date, you cannot compete with the company in any manner."

I let that soak in for a moment. I asked myself why I would sign such a document. Surely I could get out of it.

"People sign these things all the time," I said flippantly. "There is always a way around non- competes and besides, they never hold up in court." I bluffed, not really knowing what I was talking about.

Before acknowledging my retort, Mr. Rooker shuffled in his seat, confidently sitting back as he crossed his legs. He picked up his pen and rolled it between his thumb and index finger. "For a non- compete to hold water, it has to be signed with consideration. Do you understand what that means?" he asked.

"No, not really. But I'm sure you're about to enlighten me," I shot back.

Mr. Rooker disregarded my tone. "Consideration means you're offered something for your non- compete in the form of money, equity in the company, or any other type of compensation."

"I was never offered anything." I protested.

"On the contrary, Mr. Backerton. You were offered your salary with performance bonuses."

"But isn't that expected?"

"Most certainly, and according to your contract you accepted the terms of the non-compete."

"And where does it state that?"

Mr. Rooker placed the pen back on the table and flipped through the pages of the contract, stopping about halfway through.

"Page 15, paragraph 15-4. Do you want me to read it to you or would you like to read it yourself?" he asked, matching my sarcasm with an equally condescending tone.

I pulled the document from his hands, and quickly scanned the paragraph. The second sentence read:

15-4 "Salary and commissions shall be deemed sufficient to provide the necessary consideration to satisfy the conditions of the non-compete."

My necktie suddenly felt like a noose.

"Okay fine, you got me there. So I find something for the next two years, then I reintroduce the partition project to the industry in a different wrapper," I snapped.

Mr. Gilmer pursed his lips and shook his head. He looked at Mr. Rooker and nodded. "I'm sorry Chance, but that's not a possibility either."

"What do you mean? It's my idea. You're telling me I can't have the idea that came from my own brain?"

Mr. Rooker shuffled through the contract again. "Do you want me to read this section, or do you want to read this yourself?"

"Just read it!" I snapped, irritated.

"Any and all ideas, products, or procedures that are introduced during your time of employment become the property of the company."

I sat in silence. I didn't know what to do. How was I going to explain this to Kelsea? I wanted to burst into tears. I made a lot of money, but we had been putting most of it into our home. What am I supposed to do now, sell my new home? As I felt my world shattering around me, I suddenly had one final idea.

"That contract isn't valid if you terminate me under these circumstances. You can't take away my ability to work. There has to be some type of protection. My termination isn't based on under- performance. If anything, you're letting me go because of my over-performance. There has to be a clause somewhere." I was grasping at straws, and they knew it.

Mr. Gilmer looked at Mr. Rooker for the last time as the attorney began shuffling through the document again. I didn't want to hear what the contract said. It was obvious they were covered. At that moment I vowed to have an attorney review any other contracts before I signed anything again.

"Do you want me—" Mr. Rooker started.

"Yes, Mr. Rooker, please demonstrate your phenomenal reading skills one more time," I interrupted, my voice dripping with sarcasm.

Mr. Rooker read one last sentence. "Termination is defined as any reason the employee is not working for the company."

"I was present when you signed this, Chance," Mr. Gilmer interrupted. "We went through this together."

"I guess when the money is being flashed in your face, it's hard to concentrate on the details." I spoke louder than I probably should have and I felt the blood rushing to my face.

"That's irrelevant," he said. "You signed the contract with full explanation, and your initials are at the bottom of each page as a witness that you read all of them."

"Yeah great, you got me," I conceded angrily.

Ms. Morison was the last to speak. "We're sorry for all of this, but the board has made a decision. It is the duty of this committee to make sure the decision is carried out. Is there anything else you would like to say?"

"Yeah, there is. I'm upset and frustrated and am being punished for making the company money. I don't understand how this works. I put together the most successful project the company has ever seen, and I get the shaft. I just feel bad for Bob Sparks. He has five kids for crying out loud."

"Bob will retain his employment," Mr. Gilmer said quietly.

"WHAT? Bob 'I don't work late' Sparks is keeping his job?" I exploded. "That guy rode my coattails through the entire project. Why are you keeping him?"

Mr. Barnes spoke for the first time. "We're not getting anywhere with this."

I looked directly at him. "I think I deserve to know why Bob keeps his job, but I have to go? It's a simple question, and I think you at least owe me an answer," I demanded.

Mr. Gilmer slid forward in his chair. "He will continue with the project. He's assured us he can handle the details."

Clearly, this meeting was over. There was nothing I could say that would change their minds. They had me, and now they owned the last two years of my life as well. I stood and started for the door, and everyone else stood at the same time.

Mr. Gilmer put his hand out to shake mine but I stormed past him. He patted my shoulder as I passed. "You'll be okay, Chance. I have all the confidence in the world in you." His words felt demeaning, even though he seemed sincere – at the end of the day he probably was. After all, the decision wasn't his. He must be nervous because I make him look good — we'll see how old Bob makes him look now, I thought arrogantly.

I entered the elevator and hit the button for the fifteenth floor. The doors shut but the elevator didn't move. I pushed the number again, but nothing happened. I pushed the button to open the doors on the fourteenth floor where Mr. Gilmer still stood.

"I can't get up to my office," I said.

"You can't go up. You have to go down to the garage. You've been locked out," Mr. Gilmer answered.

The veins in my neck began to pound. "What about my things?" I growled through clenched teeth. "Security is packing your office. We'll have the contents sent by courier to your home tomorrow." I felt in my pocket, realizing I had left my car keys on my desk.

"I need to get my—"

Mr. Gilmer pulled my keys from his pocket and placed them in my hand, along with an envelope addressed to me. "I'm sorry Chance. Good luck." And just like that, he turned and walked away.

CHAPTER 2

What Now?

Devastated and numb, I drove my car through downtown. How could they let me go? My project had made the company millions of dollars. I'd worked for the company since graduating from college. What was I supposed to do? How would I pay my bills? I could get unemployment, but that wouldn't be enough to cover even my car payments. I made great money but we still lived paycheck to paycheck. Kelsea could go back to her nursing job, although I felt guilty when she worked at the hospital, knowing that she would rather be home with our children.

I pulled up to an intersection as the light turned red. On the corner, a homeless gentleman dressed in a torn plaid shirt and ripped jeans, sat on the curb, holding a sign. I was just a missed check or two away from homelessness myself. That deep pit in my stomach returned. What was I going to do? What would I tell Kelsea? I dreaded going home, so I passed my exit and continued on the expressway.

My bills weren't going to stop because my checks had. What could I possibly do about that now? I could get another job but my lifestyle was based on a big salary. Between my churning stomach and runaway thoughts I hadn't been paying attention to my surroundings. Once I finally snapped out of it, I realized I was thirty miles past my exit.

I decided the time had come to break the news to Kelsea. I pulled off the next exit, turned around, and headed the other way. It was close to noon; she'd wonder why I was home so early. It had been months since I'd taken her to lunch on a weekday. She'd instantly know something was wrong.

I pulled into my driveway and opened the garage door. My home was in a cul-de-sac we fell in love with on our first visit. Every lot in our neighborhood was wooded, and each house had a beautiful view of the valley below. Construction on our home took just over a year, but at the time we were building, it seemed to take forever. We were meticulous in picking out colors, appliances, countertops, brick, and everything else that goes into a home. Needless to say, the house turned out perfect for us, and we thought we would live there forever.

As I entered the kitchen, I saw Kelsea, busy making sandwiches for our girls.

"Daddy!" the girls yelled, running for me. I leaned over and picked both of them up, kissing them on their cheeks. At least I still had them. Kelsea turned to look at me with a smile that quickly vanished.

"Something's wrong. You only get that look on your face when something's wrong." She knows me all too well, I thought. I took her in my arms and kissed her gently. She relaxed a little.

"What's wrong? Why are you home so early?"

I didn't want to tell her. I didn't know how or what to say. Instead, I hung my head, embarrassed, staring at the floor. Even though it wasn't my fault, I still couldn't look her in the eye.

"I was fired!" I blurted out. I decided to lay it out and wait for her reaction.

"Fired?" she whispered. "What are you talking about? Your project is all over the news. How can they fire you?"

"The company is having financial problems and they let forty percent of the highest paying jobs go."

"You were highly paid?" she asked with a sarcastic grin. "Apparently," I replied.

"But you work so hard!" The confusion in her voice echoed my feelings.

"It doesn't matter," I shrugged. "All they care about is the bottom line."

"Well, will the bottom be any better without you?"

"I guess they think so, but they said since the Partition Project is well on its way, Bob can handle things from here. They'll be fine without me."

"They didn't fire Bob? That guy stood back and watched you make him look good."

"I know, and I voiced my concerns about Bob."

"Well isn't that a nice thank-you?" She suddenly perked up. "They gave you a severance—didn't they?" she asked, hopeful.

"I don't think so. We didn't discuss a severance." But then I remembered the envelope Mr. Gilmer handed to me. I retrieved it from my breast pocket and tore it open to find a note—and a check.

This is your final check along with the commissions for this month. We included a month's pay as severance.

"What is it?" Kelsea asked.

"It's a check."

"How much did you get?"

I turned the check over and looked at the amount. I felt some of the weight on my shoulders lift.

"Mr. Gilmer included my salary for the rest of the month plus commissions and an additional month's pay."

Kelsea put her arms around me and looked me in the eye, "Chance, this is certainly a setback. But I know you. You're not content to settle on anything. Let's try to look at this as an opportunity. I know we'll be fine.

You'll find something else. Take tomorrow to unwind and relieve some stress. Go golfing, or hike one of your favorite trails. Do something for you, then hit it hard on Thursday." She let go and pulled the check from my hand. She looked at the amount and smiled. "We're okay," as she took a deep breath. "We have some time. If we really need it, I can pick up a shift or two at the hospital."

I didn't want her to go back to the hospital. That alone was a huge motivation for me. But it was definitely a relief to know I had her support. I knew she was stressed and confused, but it was humbling to see the faith she had in me.

CHAPTER 3

An Unexpected Meeting

An entire day to myself without work! I didn't even know where to start. I thought about golf, but decided I'd take one of my favorite hikes in the neighboring foothills. I laced up my hiking boots, packed a daypack, and drove up the canyon to the trailhead. I slid out of the car just as the DJ on the radio mentioned a major accident on the expressway. I was actually happy to be hiking rather than wending my way through the rat race on the freeway.

The trail to my favorite destination, Elephant Rock, started off easy, but the terrain quickly became treacherous, turning the trail into a series of switchbacks that zigzagged up the steep slope. This portion of the trail was especially strenuous, with difficult vertical climbs. The muscles in my legs felt like they were on fire and my breathing became labored. After about two miles, the trail widened and leveled off. My only thought on my way up the switchbacks was making it to the top. I was in good shape, but anything could happen on that portion of the trail.

Once the terrain flattened out, I was able to let my thoughts wander onto other things. My thoughts immediately fell on the issue at hand. I thought of everything I know about business. My degree was in business.

The Partition Project had been easy for me. My understanding of computer networks and how they can be integrated to work more efficiently was second to none. It wasn't hard to sell the company on the project. The system basically sold itself. All I had to do was show up to the meetings.

Before going to work on the Partition Project, I had considered starting my own business; a consulting firm would be a natural fit for me. Fear had always stopped me from thinking too deeply about it. Besides, how would I raise the startup capital? At least with a corporation I had security—at least I thought I did. If I were in business for myself, I'd have the freedom to do what I wanted, when I wanted. I couldn't be terminated or laid off. But if I failed I'd have no one to blame but myself.

Lost in thought, I didn't realize how far I had hiked. I looked up to see Elephant Rock directly in front of me. I hadn't seen anyone else on the trail, but on top of the rock, someone was sitting in my favorite spot. I approached cautiously, turning to survey all sides of the trail. The day was clear, providing a perfect view down the canyon and out into the valley below.

"Beautiful, isn't it?" The voice came from the man perched midway up the rock.

I looked up at him, about to agree, but something caused me to do a double take. The man looked very familiar. At first I couldn't place where I had seen him, but then it clicked.

"Aren't you Gage Kempton?" I asked, puzzled.

"Yes I am. Glad to meet you. And you are?"

"Oh, I'm sorry. My name is Chance Backerton."

"Chance Backerton." Gage said my name thoughtfully. "Where have I heard that name?"

I wasn't sure what he was talking about. Gage Kempton was the owner and CEO of Kempton Motors, one of the largest car dealerships in the city. The man was a multimillionaire. I'd seen him on TV nearly all of my adult life.

"Chance Backerton—oh I know! Your company did some work on our computer system a few months back. Didn't I speak to you on the phone?"

I didn't recall speaking with Gage Kempton. That's a conversation I would have remembered. "I don't know—"

"No, come to think of it I'm certain it was you. We were having a problem with the mainframe conversion until I spoke with you and you walked me through it."

"I remember the conversation, but you never said your name."

"Would it have mattered?" Gage asked sitting back, an inquisitive smile crossing his lips.

"I suppose not. I would gladly help anyone. I guess I'm just surprised you would be the one to call. Seems like a job for the I.T. department if you ask me."

Gage leaned back and laughed. "Something I learned as a young manager many years ago was that you don't ask your employees to do anything you aren't willing to do yourself."

"But isn't that the reason why you have employees?"

"Of course it is. But if they know you're willing to jump in and do their job, they'll want to do their job better."

"I guess I've never thought of it that way."

"Do you have employees?" Gage asked.

"Well no, not exactly."

"The concept works for anyone. Most people naturally want to follow. As a leader I need to show the way and lead by example."

"Well, I don't have to worry about any of that right now. I was terminated from my job yesterday." I studied the ground as I realized what I'd just said. I had just told a complete stranger about my failure.

"I'm sorry to hear that. Have you started looking for something new?" Gage seemed genuinely concerned.

"Not yet. Are you hiring?" I half-joked.

"So you decided to come up here instead of looking for work."

"My wife thought it would be good for me to unwind for a day. You know, get some stress out."

Gage started laughing, "I'll bet you haven't been able to relax and you're letting this consume all of your thoughts."

"Well that's not exactly true. While hiking the switchbacks my only thought was trying to stay alive,"

"But seriously, what are you going to do?" Gage asked again.

"I don't know. I'd never really planned for this. I thought I would stay with my company forever."

Gage pointed a finger at me, "Let this be your first lesson in business –and life for that matter. If you fail to plan, then plan to fail—there are no exceptions."

"Yeah, I've heard that before."

"You heard it, but you obviously didn't listen," Gage said, lifting an eyebrow.

"I did plenty of planning for my job, but I guess it was limited to work."

"Well that job's gone. What's next?"

"I have no idea. I've thought about starting my own business." "Sounds good to me. What do you enjoy?" Gage asked.

"The profession I just left. It was my first job after college."

"Well, can you start your own business based on what you learned?"

"I could, but I'm bound by a non-compete for two years."

"Well that sounds like a dead end. I wouldn't waste another minute thinking about it. Tell me what else you enjoy then. Do you have any hobbies?"

"I enjoy the outdoors the most—hiking, skiing, golfing— and spending time with my family."

"Hmm—that's interesting."

His tone had changed from familiar to strange: Why would that be interesting?

"You mentioned spending time with your family. You know, on second thought, we can talk about that later. Do you realize the outdoors business is a multi-billion dollar industry?"

"Yes I do, and I've spent plenty of money with outdoor-equipment companies."

"Well, do you want your own business or are you content to work for someone else?" Gage folded his arms as he patiently waited for my answer. But I didn't know the answer. The question was simple enough, but the way he said work for someone else seemed forced.

"You say work for someone else like it's a negative," I responded at length.

"No, not at all. Most of the world works for someone else. I'm just trying to get a feel for what's best for Chance Backerton. Are you an entrepreneur or are you a worker bee? There's no good or bad—no right or wrong answer."

I'd never thought about it. Which was I?

"An entrepreneur is a person who comes up with his own ideas, correct?" I asked.

"Well sort of. Not only does an entrepreneur come up with ideas, but they also take on the risk of getting those ideas into the marketplace."

I decided to throw the question back at him. "Which are you? A worker bee or an entrepreneur?"

Gage chuckled. "I'm both. But I'm an entrepreneur first. Then I work like a bee to get my ideas off the ground."

I liked that answer. "You're one of the most successful car dealers in the country," I said. "How did it all start for you? I mean, when did you become successful?"

Gage nodded his head and smiled. "I often wonder that myself. I guess you'd need to define success."

"Oh c'mon—you're a multimillionaire."

"If you define success by the amount of money I have then you're right—I am successful."

"Well how do you define success?" I asked, my curiosity piqued.

"I'll answer that question another time. For now, if you'll indulge me, I'd like to tell you a story." As I nodded my approval, Gage continued. "One of my best friends got married young and had five children. His business was doing well, but that wasn't enough—he wanted to build an empire. He invested every waking moment into his business. He was out of town selling and promoting most of the time. He was never home to help his wife with the kids. He missed their ball games and dance recitals; he even missed his youngest child's first steps."

"So what happened to him? Did he achieve his goals?" I asked.

"Of course. He was focused on building an empire and his business became extremely successful."

"His business was successful. What about him? What happened to him?" I asked again.

"He became rich—very rich."

"So? What's wrong with that?" Now I was really confused. I didn't understand the concept Gage was trying to illustrate.

"I know what you're thinking Chance. He now has lots of money and the business is on cruise control. He spent years of hard work building his empire. But at what cost?"

"Cost? I don't understand."

"You mentioned your family. How many kids do you have?"

"Two daughters."

"So tell me—how long would your wife put up with you being out of town, living out of a suitcase instead of being home? What kind of relationship would you have with your daughters if you never saw them? What kind of relationship would you have with your wife if you were never around?"

I started to feel guilty about all those late nights at the office. Even though I knew it upset Kelsea, we'd never discussed it.

"There's a cost in every business. But in this case the cost was at the expense of his family. He built an empire but lost his family during the process. Is that really the way you measure success?"

I sat silent for several moments. Thoughts were racing through my head. I found myself wanting to be home with my family. Even though I had just seen them that morning, I was already missing them.

"I want to continue this conversation later, if that's okay with you?" Gage said. He stood up and walked back to the trail.

"I'd love to. Where do you want to meet?" I was flattered a millionaire would want to spend more time with me.

"Let's meet here tomorrow. But I have to give you a warning."

"A warning?" I asked, confused.

"You'll hear some things about me tonight when you get home. I'm sure it's all over the news by now. Please, no matter what you hear, come back tomorrow."

"Okay." The hesitation in my voice must have been obvious.

"Promise me," Gage pleaded.

"I promise."

"Okay, I'll see you tomorrow." Gage lifted his shoulders and let out a deep breath. I thought it somewhat strange, but quickly brushed it off.

I turned and started down the trail. I hoped Kelsea would be okay with me skipping the job hunt one more day. But I figured after I told her who I'd met, she'd be fine.

CHAPTER 4

The Accident

I pulled into the garage and walked inside to find Kelsea in front of the television set, watching the evening news.

"Hey!"

Kelsea looked up. "Did you hear the news?"

"No, I've been hiking all day."

"A fatal accident closed the expressway this morning. Gage Kempton was killed."

A wave of fear swept across my body. That couldn't be true—there's no way. I had spent the day with Gage Kempton. How could he possibly be dead? Was I going crazy? Or had I spent the day with a ghost?

"Are you sure it was him? I mean, is that right?" I asked, hoping for any other explanation.

"It's on every channel. His family is about to make a statement," Kelsea said, turning her focus back to the television.

I sat down on the sofa and watched as Gage's wife and son approached the podium, a picture of Gage behind them as a backdrop. My face started getting hot, but my hands were freezing cold. If I said anything to Kelsea she would think I'd lost it.

I started to wonder if it was all some kind of elaborate joke, but then I remembered what Gage said before I left. He knew the press would heavily report his death.

He'd asked me to come back no matter what. He practically pleaded with me, making me promise. A part of me was scared to go back. What would I find? Would he be there at all?

I debated whether or not I should say anything to Kelsea, but thought I probably shouldn't mention it—for now at least. The girls were playing in their bedroom. I couldn't ask for a better opportunity to say something about my meeting, but I couldn't bring myself to say anything. I made the decision to go back based on curiosity alone, although now I had a few questions of my own.

"I said, did you have a nice hike?" Kelsea asked loudly.

I snapped back into the present. "Yes. Why are you yelling?"

"Because you're a million miles away. What are you thinking about?" Kelsea asked.

"I'm thinking I need another day in the mountains," I said with a nervous smile.

"If it helps, then do it. Clear your mind—do whatever you need to do." She waved her hand at me, encouraging me to go.

My thoughts were stuck on Gage's story about his friend who lost his family while building his empire, and at the moment, I was thinking of Kelsea and the girls in a different way. I realized I had lost focus on them while dedicating most of my time to my job.

CHAPTER 5

Passion

I was nervous the next morning as I set out on my hike. I reached the trailhead, wondering what I was going to say to Gage. What was he doing there anyway? After I got past the strenuous switchbacks, I was finally able to think. I had enjoyed my conversation with Gage the prior day and I wondered what he would tell me today. As I approached the rock I could see Gage dressed in tan slacks and a red golf shirt. I hadn't noticed before, but he was definitely not dressed for hiking.

"Chance!" Gage quickly stood. "I'm glad you made it."

"Yeah, yeah. Before you go on I have a few questions." I wanted to get right to it, no idle chitchat. I wanted to know.

"Okay, ask away." Gage's face fell in surrender.

"You're dead!" I exclaimed. "Do you realize this? Or do I have to tell you again? YOU ARE DEAD!"

"So I made the news?"

"Every channel."

"Wow! Every channel." Gage let out a breath as if he was surprised. "Well, yes—I died in a car accident yesterday. Kind of ironic don't you think? I'm a car guy and I died in a car accident." He chuckled to himself. "Anyway, I was sent back to tie up a few loose ends."

"Loose ends?"

Gage sat down on the rock, and motioned for me to sit next to him. "One of the keys to success is helping others to succeed—teaching people how to get out of their own way. Apparently I didn't do that part so well in my life. I was told someone would present themselves to me and I'd have the opportunity to help them before I could move on."

"Present themselves?" I asked. He made it sound so formal.

"Yes, and you're the only one who has been able to see me, so I assume it's you." Gage looked up toward the sky, "Apparently my eternity depends on you. Unless I pass my secrets of success on to someone else, I am unable to continue."

I wasn't sure if I should stay and listen or run back down the trail, get in my car, and never return. What was he? A ghost? An angel? I didn't understand. Either way, I was taking advice from a dead man. I felt a strange curiosity that stopped me from running. Dead or alive, Gage was a huge success

—I could learn a lot from him. Most of the self-help books I'd read were written by people who left their wisdom behind in books. I guess this wasn't much different. I climbed up on the rock and sat down next to Gage.

"Chance, you've made a good choice. Maybe we can help each other." Gage looked at me and smiled. I saw a look of relief in his smile.

"I'm surprised you never passed any of your knowledge down to your sons," I remarked. Passing the business to his sons made perfect sense.

"I would've loved to, but their focus was on sports, not business. Neither one of them had any interest in cars." As Gage said this his mouth turned down for a moment. His disappointment was obvious.

"I suppose they found their own way. They're both successful in what they do.

Most important though is that they're happy," a smile slowly crept back over his lips.

I decided to change the subject.

"How did you get into the car business?" I asked.

"I've always loved cars. I still have the first car I ever owned. It's a 56 Chevy, and it's parked in my garage." Gage looked past me, drifting into thought as he reminisced about his old car. He just sat there for several minutes—his eyes all droopy and a small grin on his lips. "Do you have a passion?"

He asked the question so fast it startled me. Do I have a passion? I've never thought of it. I loved a lot of things, but I wasn't quite sure what he meant.

"What do you mean by passion?"

"You know, a passion — like do you have a deep emotional connection for something or someone that is almost uncontrollable?"

"Like a passion for boats or skiing?"

He snapped his fingers and pointed at me. "Yes! That's exactly what I'm talking about! That's how I feel—well, felt—about cars. My true love! I was always faithful to my wife, but my love affair with old cars sometimes caused jealousy. I loved to collect and fix them. I even had the opportunity to visit Jay Leno's garage. I lived for that kind of stuff." Gage paused for a moment. "I don't want you to think I didn't love other things—my passion had boundaries. But making my passion my life's work made working like not working at all. I felt like I played all day. New cars would roll onto my lots. I loved to sit in them and look at all the new gadgets they were equipped with. I took cars for test drives just for fun."

"You had literally any choice in the world for a car to drive. Your dealership had virtually every brand. What kind car did you drive? What did you choose for yourself?"

I asked, already anticipating his answer. Gage wore a golf shirt to work during the week—he must be a sports car type of guy or maybe he had a huge SUV.

"My wife drives an Acura MDX. I had a Chevy Suburban in the garage to pull the boat, but my car was a late-model Jeep Wrangler." Gage smiled as he sighed.

What? The guy was a multi-millionaire. He could drive whatever he wants, but he drives a Jeep?

"Why a Jeep Wrangler?" I asked, completely shocked. I thought for sure he would have driven something expensive.

"Because I loved it!" Gage took in a deep breath and slowly let it out. "It's simple enough that I could fix it myself and the top came off in the summer."

"Fix it yourself? You had shops in every one of your dealerships. And you fixed your own car?"

"Chance, you're forgetting: Cars were my passion!" Gage exclaimed.

"Okay, okay. No need to get upset. But at least tell me you had something nice."

"Of course I did. I had a Harley-Davidson."

"Now you're talking, which model? How long were you on the waiting list? What am I thinking—you probably had connections in Milwaukee?"

"Actually, I picked it up off eBay for two grand. I know, a steal right? It needed lots of work, but she ran like a champ."

Two grand? I didn't even want to know the year. One of the wealthiest guys in the country buys a used Harley off eBay for two grand. What could this guy possibly teach me about business? Bargain hunting? Or maybe frugalomics?

"Judging from the look on your face you want to know why."
"Yeah, I'm confused."

"Well my second passion was motorcycles. I loved to fix them up! That's what I liked!"

"Got it. So you are the richest man I've ever met, but you liked to drive the biggest piece of junk on the road. No problem, I get it."

"No, you're not getting it—it's passion my boy! It's all about passion. My success started from my passion for cars. Do you want to know where I started?"

"Sure, why not. I've got all day."

"Yeah, cut it with the sarcasm. Listen and you might actually learn something." He gave me a quick wink and went on. "I purchased my first car in 1973. I found it on a corner lot in the middle of my neighborhood. One thing led to another and the owner ended up offering me a job. He was looking for someone to wash the cars on his lot every day. I was excited—he paid me twenty five cents per car."

"I hope he had a lot of cars."

"I washed on average fifteen cars a day."

I did the quick math in my head. "Whoa! You made on average $3.75 per day."

A proud smile inched across my millionaire friend's lips. "Yes I did," he said proudly. "I was living at home so every penny went into buying gas for that car."

"I bet it did."

"Hey, don't forget the average price per gallon was forty cents. That $18.25 per week went a long way. And besides, it came with perks. I got to play with the cars."

"You obviously moved up. What was next?"

"Well the owner fell on hard times and had to sell the lot. A developer purchased the land, eventually building houses where the lot once stood. I was devastated because I loved that job. My old boss saw my disappointment and must have felt bad for me, because he referred me to one of his friends who owned a different car lot. I was hired on at a dealership about a mile away doing basically the same thing—but I got a raise."

"That had to make you happy. How much more?" I asked.

"He started me at $18.75 per week."

"Wasn't there a law against that? That's highway robbery."

"You're thinking of now—not then. You have to remember, that was a great wage for a sixteen- year-old! Minimum wage was $1.60 an hour. I was getting much more than that."

"So when did you start moving up the corporate ladder, so to speak?"

"I didn't. I never worked for a corporation—I just owned one. My boss was a few years from retirement and figured he would teach me the business. He brought me in and showed me how to sell.

As my passion grew, he taught me every intricate detail of all the cars on the lot. He had me read sales brochures for every model. I drove every car—listening to all of the sounds, playing with the radio, and the knobs on the dash. He taught me if I was going to be successful in sales I had to know the product I was selling. I had to be able to answer every possible question that came my way." Gage paused for a moment and looked at me. "Do you know your product inside and out?"

I thought about that for a moment. "I did, but I also created it. I learned as I went along," I answered.

"Well you were extremely competent in answering my questions the day I called you," he said.

I really did understand the Partition Project completely—I created every component that went into the system. Gage interrupted my thoughts as he continued his story.

"As my boss neared retirement, I worked up the nerve to ask him for his business. He was elated. He was hoping I would want to take over. I had the passion that was necessary to be successful. We met with his attorney and worked out a buyout plan."

I was starting to enjoy the story. "Is that when you started to expand?"

"I didn't expand right away. The first thing I did was hire two people—a CFO and a COO. I didn't go to college, so I knew even though I had the spirit, passion, and drive, I needed to surround myself with people who were smarter than me. I let them handle the parts of the business I didn't like."

"So you didn't like the paperwork?"

"No, not at all. I'm a salesman. I love the customer. Sure, I was privy to what was going on with the books, but I put a lot of trust in my top executives. In fact, they still work for me."

"So when was the time right to expand?" I asked.

"I never intended on expanding, I just got so busy. We gained a reputation for having great service at a fair price. Plus, I didn't like the game's most car dealers played. I wanted the customers to enjoy the experience of buying a car as much as I enjoyed selling them. I never thought about the money, it just seemed to roll in by doing the right things." Sadness crossed his eyes, but he continued. "Before I knew it, I had all of the major car manufacturers wanting me to represent their products. I consulted my key partners and decided to jump into different brands.

The first was Chevrolet. Before I knew it we had Ford, Chrysler, Honda, and Mitsubishi. And that was just the first year. We were so successful we acquired Saab and Mercedes a few years later. My final addition was two years ago when we added Mini Cooper."

"All of those choices and you drove a Jeep?" I joked.

"Okay, enough about the Jeep already." We both started laughing. I found his story intriguing, but I was still wondering what I was supposed to get from all this. But I continued to listen nevertheless.

"I never changed. I took care of my customers, gave them great products, and provided excellent service by going the extra mile."

"Going the extra mile—what does that mean?"

"If you had a problem with your car and it was still under warranty, we gave you a rental car while we fixed yours. It didn't matter if it took an hour or several days. Your life wasn't disrupted because your car was in the shop. If the car warranty had expired, we offered a shuttle service to take you home or to work—whichever you preferred. The funny thing is most people liked to wait."

"Why would they like to wait? If you offered the car service why would they wait around?"

"Because we have Wi-Fi and desks, printers, scanners, and leather sofas with big screens on the walls streaming every program imaginable. Last but not least, we had free food and drinks available. Our waiting rooms were like your living room, but better."

I took in all of what he said. He was all about the people he did business with. His passion was contagious. Customers bought from him because he did everything he could to make them feel comfortable about their purchase. He made buying a car an event. Even just talking to Gage was enough for me to want to buy a car from him.

"Before I knew it I had a lot of zero's in my bank account. I didn't know what to do with all the money. My wife and I spent our fair share, but we definitely had more than enough. I became passionate about something else." Gage paused for a moment, his lips quivering slightly. "We started a foundation for families with children in the hospital. We selected five families each year."

"What would you do for them?" Now I was really curious.

"Many people with kids in the hospital have insurance to pay the cost. But several don't, and they end up losing their homes because of medical bills. If you had a child with cancer, for example, the treatments, surgery, and care—it can add up to millions. Most insurance companies cap the amount they are willing to pay for a single case."

"So you paid their bills?" I asked. What a great thing this was for Gage and his wife to do! But his answer was even better.

"Nope. We paid off their mortgages. Whatever was left over was applied to their medical bills. We negotiated with the hospital on their behalf to lower their medical payments. Parents were able to bring their children to a home they owned free and clear. They never had to worry about their mortgage again, which gave them the freedom to care for their children."

"Was the hospital willing to negotiate?"

"Not at first, but we solved that issue. We helped them raise money to buy new equipment and build on additional wings. After that, they were much easier to negotiate with."

I didn't expect that answer. What an amazing thing. "So you believe it's important to give back?"

"C'mon, you're a smart kid. What do you think? Not only do I think it's important, I think it's a necessary component for success."

"How much of your own money did you give away?"

"I don't even know. But it doesn't matter. You can serve others by donating your money or your time. We did both. I don't care if you have millions or hundreds, your life becomes more balanced when you serve others."

"What do you mean by balanced?" I'd heard people talk about balance before, but I hadn't really ever thought about it much.

"I told you the story of my friend who found financial gold but lost his family in the process?" I nodded, remembering the story from yesterday. "He wasn't in balance."

"Well, what does it take to be balanced then?" I asked.

"If any aspect of your life that's meaningful is neglected because of your quest for financial riches, then your life is out of balance."

"Are you saying that being rich is bad?"

"No, not at all. I had plenty of money, but believe me when I say my life was balanced. At least I thought it was. I told my wife in the beginning the amount of time I was willing to give our business— nine hours a day.

I worked every minute of those nine hours, and then it was her time. Every day she knew when I was coming home—she could plan on it and I never disappointed her. Okay, maybe a time or two, but I always let her know if something unavoidable came up. I never missed a sporting event for one of my children. I never missed their piano and dance recitals, no matter what time of day. When I put something in my schedule I stuck to it. My family was my greatest passion and I didn't want to let them down. In fact, I heard a saying once: No amount of success can make up for failure inside the home. I lived by that."

"So balance is work and family then?"

"Yes, but don't forget your spiritual well-being. Do you pray?"

"Not really. Maybe if I really need something or I need to get out of a jam," I mused.

"Wow, you're a deep guy," Gage joked. "Do you believe in God?"

What was this, church? I wasn't sure what I believed, but I felt something must be out there—at least I hoped there was.

"Yeah, I guess I believe in God."

"He blesses us with everything, including our passions. I don't want to get all preachy on you, but your belief system is critical in balancing your success scale. It's important to be grateful for the things and opportunities we are given. I thanked God every day for my family and my ability to take care of them. Gratitude can be shown in several ways: Phone calls, cards, letters, and prayer, just to name a few. This is a very important concept.

Be grateful for the people you are blessed to be around and let them know it. Don't think for a second you're blessing them, because you will be blessed by them."

"So you don't feel that you are a blessing to those kids and their families?" I asked.

"In my mind they bless me," Gage answered. "For me, it's just the look and the feeling I get when we tell them what the generosity of others has done for them. It's a blessing for me to be an instrument in God's hands—to be able to do the things He can't do. He can bless with his spirit, but He's not going to show up and pay a bill. That's what we're here for. I believe He blessed me with the passion and resources to help those families, and I acted on that passion."

I shifted on the rock, trying to get more comfortable. I looked out over the valley to see dark clouds gathering. Conditions in the canyon can get dangerous quickly during a storm.

"Many people believe if they serve others, the reward will be personal success. I suppose that's true, but that was never our motivation. That was definitely the outcome, but never our motivation."

A crack of lighting split the sky above our heads, with the thunder that accompanied echoing off the canyon slopes seconds later. The skies had turned dark—rain was starting to fall. I looked at my watch, we had been talking for several hours.

"I better head down before the rain gets too bad." "Fair enough. Will you be back tomorrow?"

"I really need to start looking for a job."

"I'll make it worth your while. In fact, I'll share with you something of great importance— something that could change your life."

"What is it?"

"Come back tomorrow. No matter what—be here."

I slowly nodded, not really giving him an answer. As I started down the trail, rain pelted my head. I really didn't mind. My head was already swimming with the things Gage had said. I liked the idea of having my own business.

I could have returned to work for someone else, but then I'd be making a lot of money for them—why not make the money for myself and hire smart people to make money for me? I liked the idea of that much better. I was soaking wet by the time I finally reached my car. Rain was pouring down as I backed out of my parking spot and headed home, still pondering the question: What is my true passion?

CHAPTER 6

Obstacles

I was restless all night. I couldn't get the things Gage and I discussed out of my mind. When morning finally arrived I got up and showered, slipping on a pair of shorts and an old t-shirt. I was still looking for my shoes when Kelsea walked in.

"Interesting choice of clothes for job hunting," she said, her hands squarely planted on her hips.

I didn't dare tell her the truth. I mean, what would she think if I told her that I'm taking advice from a dead multimillionaire? I quickly thought of something to say.

"Yeah, about that," I answered. "I'm not quite ready to fill out applications and perform at interviews. I just need a few more days to myself."

Kelsea's face wrinkled into a frown, but her concern quickly changed into a hesitant smile. "Take a few days then. You can get started on Monday."

A wave of relief rushed over me. Hopefully that would give me plenty of time to spend with Gage. "But promise me—on Monday you'll start looking."

"I will, promise."

"Where are you going?"

"Back to Elephant Rock."

"You've been up there the last two days. I didn't realize it was that exciting."

"I just enjoy hiking. I think the mountain air helps me think more clearly."

Kelsea picked up a basket of laundry and walked out, shaking her head. "Just remember your promise," she said.

I didn't say anything. I was happy I had a few more days to spend with Gage.

I had my choice of parking spots at the trailhead. The storm the night before had really taken its toll. Fallen trees and branches were scattered everywhere, and the creek was swollen, diverting excess water downstream.

I wondered what Gage had for me today. He was adamant about me coming back. I found talking to him to be quite interesting and I was excited to hear more of his wisdom.

The storm had ripped the trail apart, making it difficult to maneuver. Water ran across and down the trail in most areas. The recipe of mountain soil and water created a thick mud, which stuck to my shoes and slowed my progress. I had to stop every hundred yards or so to clean the sticky mud from the soles of my shoes.

The first incline on the switchbacks wasn't bad, but the second was another story. I cautiously approached a section of trail that had been completely washed out, making the slope below very steep and treacherous. One wrong step could be my last. I wasn't sure what to do. There was a large gap that I would have to cross—and without rope or any other provisions it wasn't going to be easy.

I studied what was left of the trail for several minutes. The gap was only about four feet across, but if I jumped and missed I would fall over the edge. I looked up to see if there was a tree I could climb and then drop to the other side. Plenty of trees lined the trail, but there was nothing that was even close to large enough.

The slope above was just as bad; a cliff overlooked my position that seemed just as steep as the one below, so walking up and over wasn't an option either. I decided I had two choices: Go back to the car or jump the gap. I was leaning toward going back, but I heard Gage's voice echoing in my head.

A heated internal debate ensued—heights just aren't my thing and the thought of jumping horrified me. Going back to the car would be much easier, but then the day would've been wasted. Plus, who knows how long it will take before the trail is repaired—with this kind of damage it could take weeks. I didn't know how long Gage would be around, and the thought of not hearing whatever else he had to tell me scared me almost as bad as the cliff. Finally, I worked up the nerve to jump. I took ten steps back and started sprinting. As I approached I slammed on the brakes—I just couldn't do it. I must've had some type of short circuit in my legs because they started trembling. I turned and walked back to where I'd started, my hands resting on top of my head. My heart pounded and my pulse raced, beads of sweat were streaming down my face. I turned my head toward the sky.

"I CAN'T DO THIS!" I yelled towards the clouds. I paced back and forth, walking up to the edge of the gap, looking over, but each time returning to safety. I did this several times, trying to work up the nerve to try again. I walked back down the trail and turned. I took in a deep breath and thought, you can do this! I repeated those words over and over again until I believed them. I started to run— faster than I had run since high school. I felt a burst of energy hit my legs. As I began planning my jump, I realized I was already past the point of no return. I leaped into the air—hoping, praying, and pleading— that I would find solid footing when I landed. I dropped on the other side, my feet gripping the dirt as I quickly slid to a stop. I turned to look back at my accomplishment—waves of relief rushing over my body as I loudly exhaled.

I wasn't sure if it was adrenaline or the realization of making it, but I loved this feeling. I stopped and rested for a moment and then continued on my journey.

When I finally made it to the top of the switchbacks, my body felt worn as I came down from my adrenaline high. I sat down on a boulder and removed a water bottle from my pack. I sat back and looked at the scenery around me. I was in the middle of a beautiful forest, the wet maple leaves glistening in the morning sunlight. I was glad to make it this far.

I decided to press forward and started down the easy part of the trail, but today it was going to be anything but easy. A large pine tree had been uprooted from the wind, and was lying directly in front of me.

Maneuvering around the tree was impossible, which left me only one option—I would have to go over it. The massive tree was thick and bushy. I wasn't sure where to even begin to start my climb. I studied the branches—looking for something I could grab hold of as I methodically surveyed each fallen branch. I stepped on the limb directly in front of me and then grabbed the branch above. I repeated this until I reached the top of the large pine. I paused as I planned my next move. All of a sudden, I heard a loud crack. The limb I was standing on broke and I was tumbling down to the earth below and bringing half of the tree with me. I landed flat on my back. I began to panic—I couldn't feel my arms or legs. Gradually the feeling returned as my shock wore off, and I was able to slowly raise myself up to a seated position.

I could only image what this scene must have looked like to anyone watching. I looked around, double checking that no one was there to witness my embarrassment. I slowly stood up, feeling pretty good but noting a nice cut above my knee where my pants had also ripped.

I opened my daypack and reached for my first aid kit. I dressed my wound and continued on my journey.

I rounded the last bend to see Elephant Rock rising majestically in front of me. Because of the weather, the trip up the trail had taken extra time. The familiar person on the rock stood, waving at me as I approached.

"You made it!" Gage exclaimed.

"I barely made it."

"That was quite a storm last night—I was worried the trail may be damaged," Gage joked, a small grin on his face.

"The trail was a mess, but you piqued my interest yesterday—I want to hear the lesson that'll be worth my while."

"Okay. But first, sit down, tell me about your hike."

I recited the adventures of the morning. Gage listened intently. When I got done he looked at my muddy boots feet and started his interrogation.

"How did the thick mud on your boots impair your travel?"

"Well, the weight of the mud made it difficult to walk. The more it stuck the heavier it got, and I had to eventually stop and scrape it off. It was pretty annoying and time-consuming to stop every so often to clean it off."

"Interesting. Tell me, how did you feel when you realized you had to jump over the gap?"

"Sick to my stomach! I have anxiety around heights and my legs were shaking almost uncontrollably."

"Did you want to quit?" he asked.

"Of course! I almost did."

"Why did you try again?"

"Because you said you would tell me something that was of great value. You said it would change my life. I couldn't get your voice out of my head."

"I guess I did say that." Gage smiled as he shifted, fiddling with his position on the rock. "So you were able to jump over the gap and then you had to deal with a large pine tree that was blocking the trail?"

"Yes!" I said proudly.

"And you made it over the tree as well?"

"Well, sort of. I climbed one side and fell off the other, but yes, I made it."

Gage looked thoughtfully down the canyon. A smile crept across his face. "Today I want to talk about obstacles."

"Obstacles? What do you mean by obstacles?"

"Just like the obstacles you encountered on your way up here. I told you I wanted to share something that would change your life. You're young and you'll encounter many obstacles on your journey through life. Some will be mental and some physical. All told, you were able to overcome three obstacles on your way up here. Actually four, as you obviously convinced your wife to allow you to skip job-hunting for one more day. You set your mind and visualized reaching your goal. Were they easy?"

"No, not exactly."

"Okay, and how did you feel when you finally reached the rock?"

"I felt great. I'm glad I continued forward."

"If you had quit and turned back for your car the feeling of accomplishment you are having right now—it would've never been felt. Instead, you'd be feeling quite the opposite. Frustration and discouragement would have hung over your heart just like the mud clung to your boots. And what's worse, you would've never known the difference. Both frustration and discouragement are success- killers, Chance. Is it normal to get these feelings from time to time? Of course it is, but you have to ask yourself what you'll do to chase them away.

You can't allow frustration and discouragement to loiter in your mind. They must be scraped off immediately."

"I understand what you're saying, but that's a lot easier said than done."

"Is it? Are you sure?"

I thought for a moment. I felt as if he was asking me a trick question. "Don't you find it difficult to chase those feelings away?" I responded.

"I did at first. But I quickly learned if you want to play in the arena of success, you must learn to control your thoughts. The human mind is much more powerful than you can imagine. Your thoughts literally control your actions.

"I spent some time working with people in Cleveland's projects. Very few people are able to extricate themselves from the projects. Once there, they begin to think life doesn't get any better and accepted living in poverty is the hand they were dealt. If you think that way long enough, your mind will not only believe it, but it will interact with your actions in such a way that you'll be stuck living a life of poverty."

"So what did you do when frustration and discouragement show up?"

"Before I answer, let me first ask you another question. Do you think frustration, discouragement, and other negative emotions are considered obstacles?"

I lingered on the question, thinking about what Gage asked before I answered. I realized I had a question of my own.

"Do you think these emotions come to our minds because of our obstacles?" I asked.

Gage leaned back on the rock and pondered my question for a moment, and then smiled. "Good question, I like how you're starting to think. Yes Chance, I think you're right.

However, I believe that obstacles compound in such a way that the average person will quit—therefore negative thoughts and feelings appear as obstacles that must be overcome."

"Okay, now you're getting deep. What did you do when you became discouraged? I mean, it must have happened to you at some point, right?"

"What can I say? I'm a car guy. I hopped behind the wheel and drove somewhere to escape. I loved driving up the canyon. Nature is the master teacher and has a way to calm and soothe my soul. The mountains have a way of bringing clarity to my mind. The negative thoughts and emotions always seemed to work themselves out, especially when I'm not willing to give up my ultimate goal. The longer I think about obstacles the smaller they become. A focused mind will always find a way. I love admiring the mountains and the beautiful creatures that inhabit them. Take a look around—it is truly breathtaking."

"I know what you're talking about. That's why I came here the day I was fired. This is where I come to escape," I agreed.

"So you already know what I'm trying to impress upon you. Before you answer my next question, I want you to think long and hard before you respond. Losing your job means you have encountered a large obstacle that has blocked your immediate success.

Now think about this. Deep down inside is there something—a feeling of sorts—that is telling you everything is going to be fine?"

My mind went back over the day I was fired. I felt many emotions that day, the most prevalent among them anger. I was upset with the company for stealing my project and even more so for letting I go. I was angry with the board for taking away my ability to support my family. Even though I was upset, these feelings were just the surface. Deep inside I knew that everything would work out for the best.

"If I peel through the different layers of emotions, I know I'll be fine. There's no doubt in my mind," I answered finally.

"I can't tell you how important it is that you hold on to that realization Chance," Gage responded. "You are what you think and feel, and you know you'll be fine. If you dwell in positive thoughts you'll live a life of prosperity. If you dwell on the negative, that's what you will receive, living a life of discouragement and despair. Which would you rather have?"

Just as I was about to answer Gage's latest question, I noticed a young man coming up the trail. His hiking shorts revealed he was walking on a prosthetic leg. I wondered how he was able to maneuver over the gap and past the pine tree. What's more, he walked with a limp, which made every step look like a challenge. I wondered what his story was.

"Someone's coming," Gage exclaimed.

"Yeah, I see him. I wonder how he got around the gap and climbed over the tree."

"I don't know—why don't you ask him?"

"Will he be able to see you?" I asked.

"No—only you can see me. Trust me that fact was made very clear. That's how I knew you were the one I was supposed to talk to. You were the only one who has been able to see or hear me."

"Hello up there!" the man greeted me.

"How's the hike?" I waved back, noticing that he didn't have any mud on his boots.

"It's beautiful! I was quite surprised to see minimal damage on the trail, especially after last night's storm."

"Minimal damage?" I responded quickly, and a little more loudly than I'd intended. What was he talking about? I could barely make it to the rock and the guy with one leg is saying there was minimal damage?

"How were you able to cross the gap?" I asked.

"What gap?" he asked.

"On the second switchback?"

"I didn't see a gap. Are you sure it was there?"

Couldn't see the gap? Was this guy crazy? The gap was in the middle of the trail. "What about the pine tree over the trail? How did you manage to climb over it?"

"Sorry buddy—didn't see a pine tree. Are you okay?"

"Of course I'm okay. Are you?"

"Whoa! Sorry, I didn't mean to upset you. My name is Nicholas, by the way."

I didn't mean to seem upset, but I guess I did appear a little irritated. I decided I'd better play it cool.

"Good to meet you Nicholas, I'm Chance and this is—yeah, the name's Chance."

I almost slipped and introduced Gage, which made sense at the time. After all he was standing next to me.

"Is someone else up there?" Nicholas asked confused.

"No, it's just me. Why do you ask?" But I knew exactly why he asked. His forehead wrinkled and his lips pursed, but Nicholas—trying to appear friendly no doubt—smiled and shrugged his shoulders. I knew he thought I was nuts, which in all fairness, was pretty accurate, as I was wondering the same thing.

"Okay, well nice to meet you Chance. I'm heading to the top so I'd better get going."

"Sure. Have a good day."

I watched Nicholas continue his climb, struggling up the trail until he'd completely disappeared. Gage was shaking, no longer able to control his laughter. I didn't think it was very funny.

"I don't get it," I exclaimed.

"What don't you get?" he asked still laughing.

"The trail was a mess when I hiked this morning. He didn't encounter any of what I did."

"What did you notice about Nicholas?"

"What do you mean, what did I notice?"

"Did you notice something different about him?"

I thought for a moment and then remembered his leg. "He had a prosthetic leg," I reflected.

"As you hiked the trail this morning you overcame three obstacles that slowed your progress and threatened to disrupt your journey."

"Yeah—I know, we've already discussed this. I was happy, I didn't quit, and I made it regardless. What does that have to do with anything?"

"Nicholas is different than you—why would his obstacles be the same as yours?"

"Are you saying that those obstacles were just for me and now the trail is clean and the gap repaired?"

Gage smiled, his gaze lingering out over the valley and then back at me. "I don't know if those obstacles have been removed for you, but I do know if they remain conquering them for a second time will be much easier. You've already conquered them once. You've learned the best way to prevail— will they be there? Most likely, but now they will be of no consequence to you."

Gage was right. I thought of all the times in my life when I had to overcome obstacles—once I did they became much easier. Learning to ride my bike, for instance, came to mind. Balancing was difficult and it took me hours to not fall over. I remember moving about five feet or so and falling to the side. I was glad my dad had the forethought to make me practice on grass. But I finally got the feel and away I went. Once I learned to balance on two wheels I never forgot—or as Gage would say, what I once saw as a difficult obstacle was no longer an obstacle at all.

"Chase, I want you to do me a favor."

"Sure, anything."

"I have accidentally created a problem for my wife—other than dying, of course. I want you to attend my funeral."

"What? I don't know your family."

"But I consider you a friend. I want you to attend as my friend."

I didn't feel comfortable going. What would I do? What would I say to people if they asked how I know Gage?

"But that's not the favor."

Not the favor? What could he possibly have in mind?

"I'm almost certain my wife will have a gathering at our house after the service," Gage said taking a deep breath. "I want you to tell her something for me."

"So let me get this straight—you want me to approach your wife and tell her I have a message for her. Not just any message, but one you gave me today—because I've been talking to a dead man."

"Well, of course it doesn't sound good when you say it that way. Just tell her you're a friend of mine and we have done a fair amount of business together."

"And what do you want me to tell her?"

"In our closet at home there's a box. It contains some papers she needs. By now she's probably frantically looking for them. I was cleaning out my office and placed them in the closet."

"So you don't think she will find it strange a friend you do business with knows where you keep important papers in your home? Because as your business associate I'd know a complete inventory of your house, correct?" There was no way I was doing this.

"Okay, okay, you're right. She might find it extremely odd." Gage put his hands over his face. I wasn't sure what he was doing.

I couldn't tell if he was sad or just thinking, and he started to shake his head. "She has to find those papers. I'm sure my attorney has asked her for them by now."

"What are they?"

"My life insurance information, as well as my trust documents among other things."

"Doesn't your attorney have copies?"

"I insisted on having the only copies. I'm funny that way."

"You're funny in more ways than just that. Fine!" I couldn't believe I had agreed to do this, but I figured she would never see me again so what the heck?

"Fine what?"

"I'll do it—I'll find an opportunity to talk with your wife and try to convey the message without sounding creepy, if that's even possible."

"Chance, thank you so much—you don't know what this means to me. Oh, and one other thing."

"Don't press your luck Gage."

"Please—tell her I love her. I don't remember if I told her before I left the house that morning," he said, pressing his lips tightly together.

I could see he was disappointed in himself. "Of course I will, Gage. Of course I will."

CHAPTER 7

Remembrance

Sure enough, my obstacles were still there, waiting for me on my way down. But as usual Gage was right. Now that I knew how to overcome them, I didn't have nearly the delays back down the trail as I'd had on the way up.

I was jolted back to reality as I suddenly realized Gage's funeral was the next day. I wanted to ask Kelsea to go, but ultimately I decided against it—I didn't have to be a rocket scientist to know she would definitely find that strange.

The next morning I walked into the kitchen dressed in my black suit. "Job hunting today?" Kelsea asked when she saw me.

I didn't want to lie to her, but I didn't want to tell her either. Instead of making something up I quickly answered back, "Yeah, something like that."

Kelsea moved close and kissed me on the cheek, "Good luck. You'll do great!"

I gave her a hug and headed for my car. As I drove away I felt the butterflies again in the pit of my stomach. I honestly had no idea what I was going to say to Gage's wife.

I thought she might even call the cops when I told her I'm Gage's friend who just happens to know where all of his important documents are hidden.

Lost in my thoughts, the twenty-minute drive to the church went quickly.

I drove through one of the city's most exclusive neighborhoods. The homes were enormous, every yard well-manicured and meticulously maintained. Expensive cars were parked in the driveways. The church sat at the end of the block. I fought the urge to flip a U-turn and hightail it home as I searched for a parking space. As I started walking toward the doors, my anxiety seemed to actually press into my neck the closer I got.

Inside, I was greeted by an elderly gentleman. He ushered me toward a room that held the casket.

Could it really be this easy to get into Gage's funeral? I muttered under my breath.

Apparently, a brief visitation would precede the funeral. I thought this might actually work to my advantage. I could talk to his wife now and not have to stay for the service. Entering the room where the casket lay, I felt somber. A massive line of people waited to pay their condolences to Gage's family. I felt uncomfortable, seeing the devastation that Gage's death had caused his family— particularly his wife. I realized that I'd only been seeing how Gage's death benefitted me. I'd completely ignored the heartbreak and anguish of his family—the feeling was intense. I'd only known Gage a few days, and other than TV commercials, I'd never seen him "alive"—if dead is what you'd call the state of limbo he seemed to be in now. Regardless, I felt like I had known him much longer.

My heart sank with the sudden realization that Gage hadn't actually told me his wife's name. I remembered having heard it, but I was nowhere near sure. I waited patiently as the line slowly limped along and reached the family receiving line. Gage Jr. stood next to Gage's wife. I looked down into the casket to see Gage's lifeless body, eerily quiet and motionless. A feeling unlike anything I had ever experienced came over me as I looked down at him—it felt strange to think that I'd been talking to him every day since his death.

Gage's wife stretched out her hand towards me and asked my name. "My name is Chance Backerton. I'm a business acquaintance of Gage's," I managed back.

"It's so nice of you to come," she said, her voice breaking. I felt for her. Just a few days ago this beautiful woman literally had it all. And now she just looked so sad. My empathy for this woman I didn't know overcame my anxiety with my situation. She had lost so much in so short a time. I wanted to tell her everything—that I'd been talking to her husband for the last few days, how much I was learning from him, and how much he was helping me. I wanted to comfort her, but not knowing what to say, I had to improvise.

The perfect sentiment suddenly came to me. Gage had asked me to tell her two things and one of those seemed perfect right now.

"He loves you so much."

Her eyes widened, the stream of tears blocked for a moment. In that moment, her name also came into my mind.

"Janice, Gage loves you," I spoke these words as confidently as possible.

This let loose an invisible barrier that was holding back her tears as they once again spilled down her cheek. "You say that as if he's still here," she said.

"I know he is, Janice. I know he is."

She gave me a hug and held me tight. I felt a little uncomfortable for a moment, but my apprehension quickly melted as I remembered I was sent here as an instrument in the hands of Gage—or God—or whoever. She pulled away from me and looked me square in the eye.

"Thank you so much. I needed to hear that. For the first time since I got the phone call and found out about Gage, I have the feeling everything is going to be okay. Thank you Chance—thank you for that beautiful sentiment.

I can't begin to tell you what it means to me."

"You're welcome, Janice."

"Please—I'd like it if you would come by the house after the service. I'd like to speak with you some more, if that's okay with you?"

"I will, thank you," I quickly replied.

"I'll see you later then," Janice said. She smiled at me and turned her attention to the next person in line.

I walked into the church and found an open seat. The pew was made of a beautiful oak hardwood, finished with a dark stain. The room was filled with flower arrangements and plants. Gage had obviously touched many lives. The pews were filled with the most influential people in the city, including the mayor and governor.

A gentleman stood up to the pulpit and asked for the audience to rise. There was a massive shuffling of feet as everyone stood and watched as the casket was wheeled into the chapel, followed by the Kempton family. This ceremony was somewhat new to me. The only funeral I'd ever attended was for my Aunt Kelly, who died of cancer.

I didn't think I was supposed to enjoy a funeral—maybe enjoy isn't even the right word—but the remembrances were mesmerizing, with each speaker eulogizing Gage as a wonderful father, husband, community member, and friend. They also spoke of how he excelled in pretty much everything he did, how he was honest in business and treated his employees with the utmost respect, how he never took no for an answer, and how he always went the extra mile.

When things got tough, he would try that much harder. He overcame many obstacles and roadblocks to build a legacy that would provide not just for his family but also for generations yet to come. Everyone spoke of how much they would miss him.

I felt closer to Gage just by being there. I couldn't wait to get back to Elephant Rock to relate what was said to Gage—it was truly heartwarming. The most heartfelt remembrance, however, was given by his wife. She wasn't listed on the program, but after everyone else had spoken, Janice approached the podium. For a while, she just stood there, perched at the podium as she studied the audience, wringing a tissue with her hands. She dabbed her eyes and started to speak:

"I just wouldn't feel right if I allowed today to slip by without standing up and talking about Gage. He was truly a gift to me. He lived his life in a way that was an inspiration to many, especially to our family. Even though our boys weren't interested in the business, he was so proud of their accomplishments.

"Gage wanted his family to be happy. He was able to achieve much success, but his family always came first. He never missed a game or a recital, from the time the kids were three years old up until the end. He worked late nights and early mornings so he could be there for us. He enjoyed his job. He told me he never went to work— he went to play. He loved cars; almost as much as he loved the people he worked with. He was very giving and helped people who had children in the hospital. He paid off several homes and helped people pay their medical bills. He was a family man first, a philanthropist second, and a businessman third. We will miss him dearly."

Janice thanked everyone for their attendance and returned to her seat. She had given a wonderful tribute to Gage. Although the entire funeral was basically the same, her words had been echoed by everyone. If anything, I wanted to be remembered this way—but I had a feeling that if I could achieve half as much I'd feel successful.

As we left the chapel, I followed a caravan of friends and family back to the Kempton residence. Their home was huge, with a beautiful cobblestone driveway that wound up to the garage.

Ten garage doors lined the outer circle of a large courtyard. "Well Gage, so much for only having a beat-up old Jeep," I said softly.

As I walked toward the front of the mansion, I noticed the last garage door was open. I stepped inside—the sight was nothing short of incredible. Dozens of cars filled the garage—both old and new: Sports cars, luxury cars, and old classic cars. "Gage was holding out on me," I said softly chuckling to myself.

"I'm sorry—what did you say?"

I spun around to see Janice standing there.

"I—umm—well Gage had only mentioned to me he had a late-model Jeep, a Harley, and something to pull your boat with."

A rare smile lit up Janice's face. "Well he did, but that old Jeep was his favorite. He drove that thing everywhere. Unfortunately, it was totaled in the accident. The rest of these cars are his collection—Gage loved collecting cars."

"I'm sorry Janice. I shouldn't have come in here uninvited."

"Chance, its fine—don't worry. He would have loved for you to see his babies."

I walked in and looked around. The garage floor was constructed of beautiful stone tiles. An old- fashioned gas pump stood in the center, with vintage signs and posters hanging on the walls. The cars were lined up perfectly; lights shone down on each one individually. I took a few moments to gaze longingly at the cars as we walked slowly toward the door.

"Come inside. There's someone I want you to meet," Janice said.

I followed her inside, walking into a large foyer with marble floors and a beautiful curving staircase leading up to the second floor. A crystal chandelier hung from the ceiling. The sounds of dishes clanging and people talking emanated through the house. The kitchen was bustling with a flurry of people preparing food. Hors d'oeuvres were already set out on a large table.

Janice walked up to a man who looked familiar to me.

"Donald, this is Chance. He's a friend of the family," Janice said, introducing us.

I liked the sound of that—a friend of the family. Once she said his name, I instantly realized who he was.

"Glad to meet you Chance, I'm Donald Shelby."

"The pleasure's mine."

Donald Shelby was the vice president of Kempton Motors. He was Gage's second in command. Janice smiled at us.

"Well then, you two have a nice time," she said, patting me lightly on the shoulder as she turned to greet another group of guests.

"Are you here alone?" Donald asked. "I am. My wife couldn't make it."

"My wife made it to the funeral, but our son is playing in a golf tournament this afternoon, so we had to divide and conquer, so to speak."

"I know what you mean. My wife is home with our little girls."

"How many kids do you have?" Donald asked. There was something about him that instantly made me feel comfortable—something about the way he carried himself.

"Two girls, five and three."

"So you're just starting out," Donald said, chuckling. "My oldest graduates from college this year. And my youngest is a junior in high school."

"I guess we'll get there soon enough."

"Time goes by fast. They'll be out of the house before you know it. Enjoy them now, while they still want you around," Donald said patting me on the shoulder. "Tell me Chance, what do you do for work?"

"My company suffered a few cutbacks recently. Unfortunately I was let go, so I'm currently out of work."

"I'm sorry to hear that. What line of business were you in?"

I remembered what Gage had said about the partitioning they did to their systems not too long ago.

"I think you're using my brainchild at your dealerships."

"Really? And what's that?"

"I did the partitioning on your mainframes."

"Oh did you? Our system works perfectly. The partitioning software was your brainchild?"

"Yes, it's kind of hard to believe they let me go, isn't it?" I said sarcastically.

Donald's answer surprised me. "No, not at all. That's how huge corporations work. It's all about the stockholders. That's why Gage was always reluctant about going public. I don't think I'll ever allow the company to go that way. Our board thinks we should, but I don't want to give up control to stockholders. They don't know how to run our business—we do."

"Did the board try to force Gage to go public?"

"They couldn't force him, but it's been recommended several times. Tell me Chance, do you have any other ideas you're working on?"

I thought about Donald's question for a moment before responding. I'm the type of person who sees a problem and tries to solve it. Once I started, the Partition Project had consumed me—I hadn't thought of anything else.

"I don't have anything in mind, but that's not the way I think. If I see an issue that is causing inefficiency my mind just goes to work to find a way to solve it."

Donald pulled a business card from his jacket, "Give me a call Monday, Chance. I think we may have something for you and I'm interested in speaking with you further."

As I took his card my heart leapt. I had no idea what have something for you meant, but it sounded exciting. At least I could report back to Kelsea I'd lined up an interview.

"Thanks Donald. I'll call for sure."

Donald smiled as he politely excused himself, quickly disappearing into the throng of guests as he headed into a different room. I was so excited about the possibility of working for Kempton Motors, I had almost forgotten about my task. I needed to talk to Janice. I began looking around for her—she couldn't have gotten far. I started to wade through the sea of people, scanning the room and thankful my height allowed me to see over the crowd. I finally spotted Janice talking to a woman in the next room. I kept an eye on her, patiently waiting for them to finish. I moved toward her as she ended her conversation. I hurried over to Janice and tapped her on the shoulder.

I didn't know what I was going to say—I was struggling for the right words to use. I didn't want to seem crazy, but Gage had made it clear he needed my help. I hoped the right words would spontaneously come to me again.

"Janice, can I have a moment?"

"Of course Chance, what is it?"

"This is going to sound strange, but—well—I spoke with Gage about a week ago and he'd mentioned he had cleaned out his desk. He told me he was placing some very important papers in the closet. He told me to remind him that they were in a brown box on the closet shelf. I hope I don't sound crazy, but given what happened, I thought it wouldn't hurt to mention it," I shrugged, trying my best to seem indifferent.

Janice looked back at me with a puzzled look, but quickly excused herself, telling me she'd be right back. I watched her walk up the large staircase in the foyer—there was a spring in her footsteps that hadn't been there before. Several minutes went by before she returned with a stack of papers in her hands. She looked around for a few moments and then walked over to an impeccably dressed older man. She handed him the papers, which he carefully leafed through.

It was hard to miss the look of relief on Janice's face as he finally nodded his approval. She exhaled deeply. I tried my best to act like I'd missed the whole exchange as she walked back over.

"I can't tell you how relieved I am to find those papers! How did you know?" I couldn't tell if Janice's question was serious or a joke, so I played it cool.

"Know what?"

"How much I needed those papers. I was frantic when I wasn't able to find them. Thank you so much for paying attention! But most of all thanks for telling me."

I was elated. I was glad I was able to help Janice—her sadness was still very apparent, but there was a shimmer of hope in her eyes also.

"So did you like Donald?" she asked with a smile.

"Yes! In fact, we're meeting on Monday. He thinks they may have something I can help with."

"I was hoping something like that might happen. Gage was always looking for bright young people. I knew right away if you were business acquaintances, he was probably trying to recruit you. Donald will pick up where he left off."

She smiled one more time then turned and walked away. I felt the urge to tell her I've been meeting with Gage—I wanted to tell her I had never actually met Gage until after his death. I realized I'd spoil everything if I told her, and she'd think I was completely crazy. Plus, what good would it possibly accomplish? I was the only one who could see Gage—he'd told me so himself. I didn't want to mess up meeting with Donald either, so I restrained myself and left, excited to report back to Gage about the day's events. I hoped he would be happy.

CHAPTER 8

Challenging the Comfort Zone

The following day, I made it up Elephant Rock's trailhead in record time. The trail had been repaired and not even the switchbacks could slow me down.

"So how was it?" Gage asked in an animated tone.

"Wonderful!" I blurted out quickly, unable to contain my excitement.

"My funeral was wonderful? I mean, it wasn't sad or anything?"

"Yeah, sorry. Of course it was—your family is devastated. I meant it was wonderful for me."

"I'm glad you took a moment to at least shed a tear," he sarcastically shot back.

"You know what I'm talking about."

"Of course I do, that's why I sent you. Did you do what I asked?" Gage asked with wide eyes.

"I'm happy to report both tasks were a complete success."

A smile crept across Gage's face. I wanted to know what he was thinking.

"I assume you met Don?"

"I met Donald Shelby—"

"That's him. I guess I'm the only one who calls him Don," Gage said, chuckling to himself.

"What's so funny?"

"Don and I go way back. I first hired him because he's one of those guys who's much smarter than me. I had all the ideas but he had the practical answers for how to make them a reality." Gage paused for a moment, and raised his eyebrows. "This will sound strange—but it was almost like we were one in thought. He understood my vision. Our thoughts were harmonious with one another. We didn't always see eye to eye, mind you, but when we disagreed we sat down across from each other and calmly debated it until we found a solution we could agree on."

"Sounds kind of like a marriage."

Gage laughed heartily. "Really? That's how your marriage is? You argue with your wife, trying to prove you're right and she's wrong—and you sit there, going back and forth until you come to an understanding?" Gage looked at me and started laughing even harder, almost uncontrollably. "Every once in a while my wife would let me win an argument, but generally she had the final say."

"I meant the one in mind part."

"Okay, don't strain yourself kid. But I'll give you that one."

He was making fun of me, no doubt about it now. I didn't like it. He was right, but that didn't matter. He must have seen me getting frustrated, as he quickly shifted the subject back to the favor he'd asked.

"Did you tell Janice where to find the papers?"

"Yeah I came up with a good story. She retrieved them from the closet and took them to an older gentleman. I assumed he was your attorney. He nodded and she thanked me profusely."

"Good job! And the other one?"

"I told her you love her. She was standing at the head of your casket. She gave me a hug. It was actually a special moment—I think it was exactly what she needed to hear."

I looked to see tears streaming down Gage's cheeks. "I'm going to miss those hugs."

We sat in silence for a while as the sounds of nature sang to us. Eventually Gage composed himself and became talkative once again.

"So how did you feel? Were you scared to speak with her?"

"I felt very anxious—I was afraid of how she would respond." "Did your fears melt away as you started talking to her?"

"Yes, and it didn't take long."

"And you were able to accomplish your goal?"

"Of course. I already told you that."

"I know you did, and I'm glad. I'm proud of you. I knew this task would be difficult. Doing uncomfortable things isn't easy. In fact, I wondered whether or not you could do it."

I hadn't thought of it that way. I guess the situation was uncomfortable, but I did it out of loyalty and friendship. Plus, I knew Gage needed the help.

"Chance, there will be many times in your life where the need will arise for you to step out of your comfort zone. There's no way to progress if you stay in your comfort zone and only do what is comfortable. This is true for business and life. For example, I have a friend who sells insurance. When he first started he was afraid to call prospective clients."

"What's so scary about phone calls?"

"It's not the calling part that's scary—it's the rejection."

"Rejection?"

"Let me ask you this. How many times have you hoped for an insurance agent to call you?"

Well never, I guess but—"

"Exactly," Gage said quickly cutting me off. "Insurance is something we all need, but we dislike being sold. Nevertheless, I'm sure you have insurance on your cars and your home—am I right?"

"Of course, insurance is required to get financing."

"You're right, but that's not the type of insurance my friend sells. He sells life and disability insurance. Both of which aren't required but are just as important. Even so, my friend knew when he picked up the phone that most people wouldn't be interested."

"So? I'm not a salesman and I'm definitely not afraid of phone calls—what does this have to do with me?" I asked skeptically.

"He became incredibly successful! Would you like to know how?"

"But you said he was terrified of rejection."

"He was, but he was able to overcome the fear."

"How?"

"By stepping out of his comfort zone. He forced himself to become comfortable with making phone calls. He challenged himself to pick up the phone at the same time every day. He asked everyone he spoke with for referrals. Eventually he had gathered quite a list of names, and he picked up the phone every morning at 9 a.m. and started calling. He called for either one hour every morning. My point is this Chance: He set his mind to something and he did it. To this day, he still makes his calls every morning, at 9 a.m. sharp. Do you know what he discovered?"

"No what?"

"He discovered a pattern. He tracked his numbers. He found out if he spoke with ten people, five would tell him no, but three would give him an appointment."

"That's eight."

"Good math Einstein—let me finish."

"Sorry."

"The other two would ask him to call them back, so he would set a future date and time to call. Most of these numbers held true for him. Over time, he says he actually learned to like hearing no."

"No one likes to hear no."

"Well then, answer this question for me Chance: If you knew you had to hear 'no' five times to get five people to say 'yes,' wouldn't you want to get the five people who are going to tell you 'no' out of the way as quickly as possible?"

"Sure, I guess that makes sense. So he discovered all of that because he was able to overcome his fear of making phone calls?" It felt like I was beginning to understand exactly what Gage was saying.

"Exactly. If he had never stepped out of his comfort zone he would have quit. I'm sure he would have found a normal job working for someone else, but now he owns one of the largest insurance agencies in the Western states. He would never have discovered this secret, however, if he didn't step out of his comfort zone."

"Well, going to your funeral was definitely uncomfortable, to say the least."

"I know you were uncomfortable with the thought of it, but once you were there you were fine, right? And wasn't the feeling of accomplishment great?"

"It was. In fact, Donald wants to meet with me on Monday to go over a few things."

"Of course he does."

"You say that as if you knew that would happen?"

"Of course I knew it would happen. He and I think alike remember? I knew he would instantly see the potential in you. You remind me a lot of myself when I was your age."

I liked hearing that. One of the most successful guys in the city thinks I am like him? That gave me a boost on the confidence meter.

"Listen when I say this Chance. You allowed me to put you in an uncomfortable situation. Helping others isn't always easy, and in fact, it's often extremely uncomfortable.

You put yourself through all of the emotions: fear, anxiety, inadequacy—you name it.

However, you did it for me, and I am extremely thankful. But I want you to think about you. What did this exercise reveal to you? Did it help you?"

I wasn't quite sure what Gage was after. In my mind, this exercise was all about Gage, and I was happy to do it. I did it to help him, not the other way around.

Gage continued before I was able to voice my thoughts. "Now you know you can overcome any of these feelings—you can accomplish anything. In fact, I want you to remove the word can't from your vocabulary. Obstacles will always exist. Whether they are physical or mental, remember, they are still just obstacles. You've broken them, just like you did on your trip back down the trail a few days ago. The obstacles remained but they looked different. Now they are nothing but minor setbacks you can easily conquer."

I knew Gage was right. Of course, I knew obstacles always existed, but I hadn't ever thought of them in this way. I had always made it a practice to try to overcome obstacles, but I was also allowing my obstacles to control me. I had treated them as excuses. It's much easier to excuse failure than to admit you have failed.

"Chance, tomorrow I want to go over something very important. I'd like to help you prepare for the meeting with Don."

"Seriously? That'd be great! Any help would be appreciated."

Gage smiled and placed his hands on my shoulders. "We'll make sure you do great! See you tomorrow."

I walked down the trail, my mind spinning. I felt ready for whatever Gage tried to throw at me. My confidence surprised me. I wasn't sure what was ahead, but I knew I was ready for it—not just on the trail, but in life as well. I was even more excited to meet with Donald.

CHAPTER 9

Facing the Biggest Challenges

An overcast sky greeted me as I approached Elephant Rock. Clouds filled the sky and rain seemed likely, which concerned me, but it mercifully remained at a distance. My hike was getting easier, I noticed, approaching Elephant Rock in what seemed like no time at all. Gage was perched in his usual spot. I wondered where he went at night, or if he just sat there. He waved at me as I approached, but I noticed his face looked grim and expressionless, almost as if something was weighing heavily on him.

"Is everything okay?"

"Sure, why do you ask?"

"It just seems like something's on your mind."

Gage started to say something, but changed his mind. He sat totally still for another moment and then looked at me.

"I said that I wanted to help prepare you for your meeting with Don, and I intend to do that, but I need to ask you for another favor first."

I hesitated before I answered. I was worried—remembering how uncomfortable I'd felt attending his funeral and delivering his message to Janice.

"Sure Gage, what is it?" I said much more confidently than I felt.

"Something very important is on the ridge top above us. Specifically, there's a box next to a large rock," Gage said, pointing to indicate a distant ridge. "Inside that box is a valuable lesson—a lesson you must learn. I want you to hike there and retrieve the contents of the box."

I slowly scanned the ridge top. Hiking there didn't appear very difficult. At least, it didn't look too far. "Absolutely Gage. I can be there and back in a couple hours," I said confidently.

"I know what you're thinking Chance, but the hike is more difficult than you think. The last half- mile is slippery shale rock and the incline becomes incredibly steep. But no matter what, you must make it there. Failure isn't an option. No matter how tired you may get, you must retrieve the lesson before your meeting with Don. Don't return empty-handed."

His tone grew serious, which made me nervous. But after our talk yesterday, I still felt up to the task. "I'll be fine, I can do this. When should I leave?"

"Did you bring a water bottle?"

"Of course. I always do."

"How about a first aid kit?"

"I have one, but do you think I'll need it?"

"You never know."

"Yeah, I'm prepared."

"Good, stay on the trail. Once you are close to the top the trail splits.

You must stay right or the trail will curve and lead you right back here. After you bear right the trail will continue for about four hundred yards before ending at a spring. Shale rock begins just beyond there. From that point to the top you make your own trail. Dangers abound on the rock so be careful."

I swung my backpack over my shoulders. I shot one last nervous look at Gage, who nodded his approval and I turned and started up the trail.

I had hiked this trail several times, but I'd never ventured as far as the spring. The hiking was easy. There were a few steep areas, but for the most part the trail was well maintained. I could feel a blister forming on my foot, but I figured I'd take care of it if it began hindering my progress.

After an hour of hiking my throat felt like I had swallowed cotton, but I could see the split in the trail straight ahead and I pushed myself to keep moving towards it. Even though I was thirsty, I felt good enough to continue to the spring. I trusted Gage's measurements and I was sure the spring water would taste better than my stagnant water bottle.

I reached the area where the trails split, taking care to bear right just as Gage had instructed me to. The trail was steepening, and my legs were beginning to feel fatigued. The air was warming up as well and I was beginning to perspire.

I could hear the sound of running water and followed it until I came to the spring. I took out my bottle and emptied it onto the ground.

I quickly filled it with the cool spring water, tipped the bottle back, and gulped the entire thing. I filled it again and sat down to rest my weary legs. The scenery around me was beautiful—the sky was gray and low clouds kissed the ridge tops. Rain was still a threat, but I paid it little mind as I noticed the ground was still sunbaked and dry. The spring water appeared to be trickling down, creating a small stream that quickly wound out of my eyesight.

I noticed the blister on my foot felt worse. I should've taken off my shoe and bandaged it so it wouldn't burst. I was sure it was too late now and tried to get my bearings as I looked over to survey the top of the ridge. Gage was right—the only thing between the top and me is a sea of shale rock.

I put the water bottle back in my pack and stood up.

The blood flooding to my foot was almost too much to bear, but getting to the top was all I could think about. I took my first step onto the shale and noted it didn't feel completely stable. I could see farther up the slope where gaps in the rock exposed deep holes.

"Well this is going to be fun," I muttered sarcastically.

I didn't want to quit, so with no other options I started up the rock. I took it one step at a time, making sure my foot was solid before I shifted my weight. As the rocks began to get larger, I was forced to jump from one to another in order to avoid the large gaps. I remembered the washed out trail and the gap I'd been forced to jump. I wondered if I would have been able to jump between rocks without the confidence I'd gotten from my experience with the gap.

I had come a long way in a short period. I thought I was making great progress, but when I turned around to check I realized I hadn't gone far at all. The sound of the spring was still vibrating in my ears.

I turned and looked back up—desperately trying to plot a course to the top. I didn't know how I was going to make it. I sat down on a rock and pulled out my water bottle. I had hiked the entire way to the spring without water, but now I'd only taken a few steps and already felt like I was dying of thirst. I took just a few swallows and placed the bottle back in my pack as I resumed my climb. I continued my ascent in the same way as before, leaping from one rock to the next. I was growing frustrated with my rate of travel, but I didn't have a choice—I couldn't move any faster.

As I continued, fatigue was setting in more and more as my water disappeared. I wished I had thought to bring a second bottle, but pushed that thought quickly from my mind as I realized the top of the ridge was in sight.

My body felt like it was on fire—every part seemed to be screaming at me to stop. I didn't know if reaching the top was as important as I thought just a few hours ago.

I felt discouraged and considered whether or not to give up and start the climb back down—it looked much easier than going up. I decided to head back and turned around, but found myself unable to take a step in that direction. I could no longer hear the dull roar of the spring; in fact, all I could hear was Gage's voice in my head, urging me to continue.

I turned around and studied the surface of the shale rock. I saw what appeared to be the steepest incline yet, but that it appeared to be the last obstacle between the ridge top and me. I slowly moved forward, completely worn out. I felt like I had nothing else to give. My mind took over, my focus on nothing other than my next step.

My heart leapt as I crested over the ridge and collapsed in the shade. I turned to look back, proud at what I had just accomplished. I didn't realize how steep the slope was until I looked back. The mountain air felt great as a breeze cooled my face.

But this was no time to relax. I realized I was only halfway and I shifted my attention to finding the box Gage had told me about. Small rocks dominated the ridge top. I saw an outcropping to my left that looked as if it could be hiding something. I had no idea what I was looking for, wishing I'd asked Gage more questions. Unless it was in plain sight, I had no idea where else to look—all I could do was wander aimlessly with my body in total pain or give up and head back down. My energy was zapped. I questioned whether I could make it back down, but I had to find the box before I even started worrying about that.

I decided to explore around the outcropping, but if I didn't find anything I would head back immediately.

I made my way, maneuvering my body slowly downwards into the darkness of the outcropping. I came to three large boulders that jutted from the ground. I dropped myself and studied the base of the first one. I could scan from my position to the other side of the chasm, but all I saw were rocks.

My eyes were slowly adjusting to the diminished light of my surroundings and as I looked down there it was—a small black box. Exhausted, I stumbled to the box and retrieved the paper inside. I was too tired to bother with looking at it—folding it and sticking it in my pocket instead. I breathed a sigh of relief, realizing I had accomplished my task. From here I just had to make the climb down.

Suddenly, I heard a terrifying shriek that made the hair on the back of my neck stand straight up. It sounded like a cat, but not just any cat—a big cat. I looked up to see large mountain lion standing less than ten yards away. It must have been stalking me, I thought as my heart rate intensified. My brain was frantically sending messages to my legs to move, but I was so exhausted nothing was responding. I knew if I didn't act quickly there was a good chance I was going to die.

A massive rush of adrenaline hit my veins, giving my worn-out body the strength to run. I took off down the slope at a full sprint—not sure which way to go and even less sure I'd make it down in one piece. The mountain lion leapt off his perch in full pursuit. Stopping to bandage my blister would've been a great idea that I was really regretting. I felt the pain increasing with every step. I prayed I wouldn't fall, but I could hear the mountain lion closing behind me. I wasn't sure which would be worse, the fall or the mountain lion, but I knew I didn't want to find out.

The thought of making it down to my wife and daughters gave me strength I didn't know I had in me. My predicament worsened as it had started raining.

The downpour wasn't substantial yet, but it was enough to cause the slippery rock to become even more slippery.

I thought I was going to lose my balance and fall at any moment, but each time I slipped, I was able to somehow regain my balance and continue on.

I passed the spring in under a minute. I longed to stop for water, but this wasn't an option as I heard the mountain lion continuing his pursuit.

A second burst of energy hit my legs as I stole a glance over my shoulder and realized I had actually increased the distance between us to around fifty feet. I was surprised my body was still working at all, not to mention that I was running faster than I'd ever run before. I hit the trail and started back down just as the rain began really pouring down, slowing for an instant as I rounded a bend to glance back.

The lion was still in hot pursuit. My heart was pounding in my chest and my lungs were on fire. Was this it? Was this the feeling of death settling upon me? Did it even matter? By this point, I thought dying may actually be less painful than tripping and falling over any one of the trail's steep cliffs.

I could see Gage facing the valley as I approached Elephant Rock. I mustered my last bit of strength to scream, hoping my voice would be loud enough to get his attention,

"Gage help me! Gage!" It came out sounding more like a whimper.

His head quickly turned to face me as if sensing trouble. Somehow, I was still running at full speed and I was coming in toward Gage's position much quicker than I was anticipating. I finally skidded to a stop at the base of the rock and started frantically climbing towards the top. The mountain lion did not intend to stop either, continuing his relentless pursuit following my path up the rock.

He jumped to the top only slightly behind me and stopped, staring me down. I stood completely still, paralyzed with fear.

Gage looked wholly unconcerned by my plight, staring at me blankly. I noticed he hadn't even gotten up and was still sitting in the same position on the rock. I tried yelling to him, but my throat had closed from dehydration and I couldn't get the words out. Gage finally moved as he quickly put his fingers to his mouth, his shrill whistle shattered the silence as it emanated throughout the valley.

The mountain lion's gaze broke from me as he looked over at Gage. He slowly walked over sat down next to him, shifting his weight back on his massive hind legs. My jaw dropped as he allowed Gage to start petting him. Completely exhausted, I collapsed on the rock. I closed my eyes and the world went black.

CHAPTER 10

Never Give Up

"Chance—Chance—wake up! Chance!"

I slowly opened my eyes. I heard Gage yelling at me but I couldn't see him. I felt groggy, like I was coming out of surgery but still under the influence of the anesthesia.

"Chance!" Gage yelled even louder, which jolted me out of my trance. The world suddenly snapped back into focus.

"Are you okay?" Gage seemed concerned. I knew I had passed out, but I wasn't sure how long I was under. My body felt completely exhausted and my throat ached with thirst.

"Water!" I gasped, my voice barely a hoarse whisper. Gage quickly pointed toward a bottle—I grabbed it and started chugging, quickly draining the bottle and collapsing again on the rock.

"How long was I out?"

"Not long—maybe ten minutes or so? I would've let you sleep, but I started getting worried."

"Where's the mountain lion?"

"Gone, back into the forest."

"I found the box. I hiked the entire way to the top and found the box," I stammered. Despite my exhaustion, I was incredibly proud to report to Gage that I'd accomplished my task. "It was extremely difficult—and I almost died—but I made it."

"That's good. Show me what you found, would you?"

I pulled the slip of paper out of my pocket and held it out for Gage.

"Open it up. Take a look," he urged. I slowly unfolded the paper and looked in horror at the blank page in my hands.

"It's blank. There's nothing here." I wasn't prepared for this. I wasn't sure what I was expecting, but I was hoping there would be something on it that would justify my trip.

Gage smiled and shook his head, "It doesn't matter, Chance—you passed the test."

To say I was irritated would be an epic understatement. "I put my life in peril—for a test?" I asked Gage in disbelief.

"Tell me how you felt when you reached the spring?"

Exhaustion overcame my frustration. I sighed and paused, contemplating how I could even begin to answer Gage's question. "Pretty good, I guess. I was thirsty." I'd start with the basics I supposed.

"And what did you do?"

"I filled my water bottle and drank the whole thing. I filled it again for the rest of the ascent, but found myself wishing that I'd brought a second bottle."

"How was the final portion of your hike? How did you feel when you reached the ridge?"

"I felt tired. Hiking up the rock wore out every muscle in my body—I didn't think I could hike any further. At one point I even started wondering if I could make it back," I said assertively.

I wasn't sure where Gage was going with this, but I needed him to understand what his little test had almost cost me. He had a small grin on his face, an indication he was getting some sort of sick satisfaction from my misery. I wasn't sure if I could suppress my anger and frustration through another round of pointless questions.

"So let me make sure I understand. I tell you there is something on the ridge top that is incredibly important and I advise you to not return until you have retrieved it. You made it to the top, but you were so exhausted that you felt like you couldn't go on—so much so that you were unsure if you'd be able to make it back down?"

"Yeah, that pretty much sums it up."

"Well then I'd just like to know one thing—if you were that exhausted, how did you find the energy to make it back?"

"Oh, I don't know. You did notice the mountain lion that was on my tail!" I yelled back at him, no longer able to keep my anger hidden.

"Yes, I did. Was the mountain lion your motivating factor then?"

"Well, don't you think you'd be motivated by a wild cat who wants nothing more than to eat you?"

Gage sat back and laughed. I couldn't help thinking that he really was getting some kind of sick enjoyment out of this.

He'd better get to the point quick, I thought, resolving that if he tried any more mind-games my next step would be back toward to my car.

"Okay, I'm sorry Chance. Do you feel better now? I understand your frustration, but just indulge me for a moment. You were so tired you actually questioned whether you could make it back to Elephant Rock, is that right? You felt so tired you couldn't go on, but you did go on—you finally found the box and retrieved the paper inside. Remember, I did warn you that the climb was going to be dangerous. The mountain lion most likely even followed you for several hundred yards before you even noticed. You didn't know he had you in his sights. Mountain lions are opportunists. He was waiting for the best possible moment to attack. But he showed himself too soon and you took off running.

But remember Chance, you had no more energy, and a huge blister on your foot. So where did that blast of energy come from?"

"How did you know about the blister?" I asked.

Gage ignored my question and continued. "Isn't it amazing how even a minor problem like a blister can fester and end up causing a great deal of pain if it's not attended to?"

I had to think about Gage's question for a few moments. I had literally just run for my life. I wanted to live and that was more important than being tired or the pain in my foot. I had no choice but to try to survive. I'd thought of everything that was important to me and used it to motivate me to keep running.

"I literally ran for my life," I answered back.

"You found the energy because you wanted to live. Focusing your mind on survival gave you the energy to continue."

"I guess—something like that. Most of all, however, I wanted to survive for my wife and daughters."

"That's an excellent motivator. And in addition to making it back, you learned a valuable lesson as well. When you have motivators you become more focused and determined in situations like today. When you get tired and feel like you can't go further, you need to realize that you still have the energy inside to move forward. No matter how worn out you are— physically or mentally—there's always more." Gage took in a deep breath then exhaled slowly.

"When things get difficult, people tend to lose focus, get tired, and give up. You can't allow yourself to do this Chance. Achieving success is also about coping with failure. You'll have plenty of failures—believe me. You have to remember that isn't the time to give up. I guarantee you'll want to but you must keep moving forward. Runners call it hitting the wall and it usually happens as they near the end of the race.

Those who don't quit and manage to find the energy to go on will finish with the knowledge that they were able to accomplish their goal."

I thought about what Gage said. I thought of all the times I had gotten discouraged and ultimately given up. I thought back to college and a project I'd started but never finished. I was taking a class that required us to make an instructional video. The assignment was overwhelming to me. I started the project but after hitting a few obstacles, I gave up and dropped the class.

"There's another lesson here as well. The mountain lion represents people who don't want you to succeed. I call them naysayers. They lurk in the forest of your life, stalking you just like the mountain lion did, waiting until you have an idea they consider crazy or disagree with. Then they attack with their negativity.

"The lion also represents your competition, both in business and in life. Some people will fight against you and try to take from you what they feel you haven't earned. They use excuses to justify to themselves why you're successful and they aren't. They tell others you fell into your success, that you got lucky. I've seen this ugly side of people several times. They say you're successful because of who you know or relied on someone else to build your business. Like the mountain lion, these people will sneak up on you from nowhere. You may not even realize their negativity until they are standing in front of you spewing their vile. Lions lurk all over the mountains Chance, but rarely will you see them. However, their tracks are unmistakable and you can spot their telltale signs—if you know what to look for of course.

"It's the same way with people—you must be prepared to ignore anyone who is negative or doesn't want you to succeed. You don't have time to deal with them.

They will sneak up and try to distract your focus and steal your vision. They will squash your dreams if you allow them to—don't let them do that." Gage paused.

"The sad thing is that this type of person has many faces. They could be a friend, family member, or maybe even your colleague. Regardless of who it is, don't allow them to get inside your head. If they don't share your vision, don't discuss it with them. If certain friends are negative and say your goals are unobtainable, or connections are necessary to be successful, please, I ask you not to listen to them. That type of person won't keep you on the right track and will ultimately derail you anytime they have an opportunity," Gage said.

"Why are people like that? Now that you mention it, I've seen it a lot. I've even been one of the people you're talking about. I try not to be and I've tried to support dreams, but sometimes it's easier to say something isn't going to work out than it is to try. It's easy to make up any old excuse, like you don't want to give someone a false sense of hope about what they will accomplish."

"You're right, but it's their dream not yours—who are you to judge? If your dreams and goals are solid in your mind, and make sense, you'll find a way to accomplish what you set out to. Allow this to happen for others as well. Their dreams are just as solid in their minds and they deserve the same opportunities for success," Gage said. "There is a law that I know of—I learned it from a friend and have watched it work in his life. I've also watched this law positively affect the lives of virtually everyone I've come in contact with. It is a little like gravity—while it remains unable to be scientifically proven, to see how we are governed by it, all you have to do is test it for yourself."

"What are you talking about?" I asked. Gage seemed enthralled with his lecture. I hung on every word, but I was tired and wanted him to get on with it.

"It's called The Law of Attraction."

"I've never heard of that."

"Have you ever heard of karma?"

"Of course I have. What comes around goes around."

"Right—and the Law of Attraction is very similar. Whatever you put out into the world is what you'll get back—in essence, we get back what we give out. There's no exception. Think of the most miserable person you know and tell me how that person acts."

"My aunt comes to mind. She seems miserable, or at least she never seems happy. She has a job she hates but she justifies it because she has to pay the bills. She was divorced several years ago and hasn't been able to make a relationship last."

"But how does she act?"

"Sad. And she acts angry all the time."

"And you just told me she's miserable, so I assume it's safe to say she's sad?"

"Yes, you could say that."

Gage sat for a moment, letting our conversation soak in.

"Now think of the opposite. Think of the most successful person you know."

I had to think about it for a moment because the most successful person I know was sitting in front of me. "You are the most successful person I know."

Gage sat back and laughed. "Okay, well then let's take me. How do I act?"

"Well—dead?" I joked.

"Yeah—not funny. Seriously, how do I act?"

"You act confident. You know how to carry yourself. You're able to articulate your thoughts, and you're a master teacher. You seem to genuinely care about others, too—but that's just naming a few of my observations."

"Thank you Chance, I'm flattered. You're right, that is how I act and who I am. The things I put out into the world, whether mental or physical, are what I attract. Does that make sense?"

I thought about it. The concept seemed simple enough, but I wasn't clear on how it actually worked. "A lot of people carry on, living happy lives and work from nine-to-five doing something they don't like. But they do it because they are able to support their families. Do you think that means they're happy?" I asked.

"Of course, Chance. They're happy because they send happiness out into the world. The poorest person in the world can still be charitable, and more importantly they can still be happy. They are sending positivity out, why wouldn't they get it back? That doesn't mean riches will just fall into their laps. I've spent a great deal of time in Mexico and South America where many of the people live in poverty. Most live in small cinder block houses with dirt floors. Some have no idea where their next meal will come from. I used to think these people had to be miserable. I was surprised after I met quite a few of these people that I found quite the opposite was true. Many of the people I met would gladly give the shirt off their back to someone who needed it.

They insisted on sharing their precious food with me—even when they didn't have enough for themselves. The children were happy and the families were strong."

"Let me explain it another way: There are two types of people in the world—victims and victors. A victim is always complaining about their lot in life. Nothing is their fault and they never take responsibility for their actions. When things don't seem to go as planned the victims always find an excuse—these people are never as successful as they feel they should be.

The opposite of that holds true for the victor. The victor sees opportunity in every situation. They see the silver lining. They see the inherent good in people, and instead of responding with jealousy, they are happy when others succeed. Most of the successful people I know all share that same common trait—they are victors. I know you've heard the saying: 'when life gives you lemons make lemonade.' Don't complain if life gives you limes instead of lemons. Nevertheless, I feel I should make one point clear. Most of the people I know who cruise through life, working the same job, making virtually the same money— these people are not failures. Quite the opposite, actually—I consider their successes by looking at the way they raise their families and contribute their time. They may or may not be of the victim mentality, but that doesn't mean they haven't found happiness. The same can be said for victors, whether or not they've found enormous success in the world, their families have likely suffered at some point along the way. On the outside they appear successful and balanced, but inside they are often miserable.

Thus, there arises a need for balance, but we'll get to that another day. I'm sure I've given you enough for the time being."

Gage's voice trailed off as he allowed me some time to reflect on what he had just said.

The Law of Attraction made sense. I thought of several people I know and mentally examined what they were putting out into the world. They are a result of what they send out. I wondered what I was— a victim or a victor. I hoped I was a victor. Even though I'd lost my job, I hoped I would be able to land on my feet. I didn't like having to rely on anyone but myself.

"Chance you have a lot to think about. It's getting late, so why don't you come back tomorrow and we'll continue where we left off." Gage's voice brought me back to reality. I looked up at the sun, realizing how late it was. I'd barely make it down to the car before dark.

"I'll be back tomorrow," I said, hurriedly sliding my backpack over my shoulders.

"We still have much to discuss before your meeting with Don. Tomorrow will be an important day."

I started back down the trail. I had a feeling my time with Gage was getting short. There was something about him—I couldn't put my finger on it, but something told me he was about to continue on to the next part of his journey. Part of me was happy for him, but another part of me was sad he couldn't stay on Elephant Rock forever.

CHAPTER 11

Balance

I parked in the lot at the trailhead and got out of my car. I looked up at the deep blue sky as I stretched my arms above my head. The temperature today was perfect for hiking. It was Friday, just three days until my meeting with Donald. I was excited to meet with him, but nervous as I was entering what might be my final days with Gage. I wasn't sure when he would leave, but I felt the time would arrive more quickly than I thought. I reached the switchbacks and thought back to how much I had hated them those first few days of hiking. They were easy now—I didn't even break a sweat most days.

Off in the distance Gage sat perched in his usual spot on top of Elephant Rock. He sat watching the trail as he awaited my arrival. He waved as I approached. I noticed he was dressed differently today. Up until now he had been wearing the same clothes, which didn't look very comfortable or well suited for hiking. He was wearing shorts and a t-shirt. He looked different, but as I got closer, I saw an unmistakable glow that was surrounding him.

"Good morning Chance."

"Good morning. You changed your clothes I see."

"I did, we're going on a hike. I wanted to make sure I was dressed appropriately."

"How far did you have in mind?" I asked still puzzled as to where and how Gage had managed to obtain new clothes.

"We'll get to the spring and decide from there."

"The spring? We're not going to the top of the ridge are we?"

I was hoping I would never have to climb that shale rock again, and Gage's answer did not disappoint.

"No, no. Today is different. Today is going to be a little scary, though."

"Scary?" I wasn't sure if I like the sound of that.

"You'll be fine. Just do what I say." Gage hopped off the rock and began to walk with me up the trail. We walked for a while in silence as my thoughts raced. Each day had brought different experiences—I was a little concerned about what exactly he had in mind.

"Chance, you said something on the first day we met," Gage said finally breaking the silence. "I asked what you enjoyed and you listed off a few things which included spending time with your family—do you remember that?"

I thought back to that day and nodded my head in agreement. To be completely honest, I'd felt a little guilty ever since we had the discussion that I hadn't mentioned my family and how much enjoy spending time with them first.

Gage's reply seemed to read my mind, "I'm not going to ask why you didn't mention them first— I'm pretty sure you've been kicking yourself for it ever since."

I nodded again as he went on. "I want to talk to you about balance."

"You mentioned balanced before."

"I know, and balance is important enough to go over again. We all need to find balance in our lives. I mentioned to you before the words of a friend, '

If any aspect of your life that is meaningful is neglected because of your quest for financial success, then your life is out of balance.' What do you think that means?"

"I guess it could mean it's possible to go too far—that our focus can become too absolute and end up taking away from the important things?"

"Exactly! Let me explain something to you. Balance is an integral component of success. You can't be married to the job. If you neglect your family, then is it really worth it? Decide when you're going to be there for them. Decide how much time you're willing to give your work and how much time you're willing to give your family. Schedule your family time and stick to that schedule. Treat it as if it is just as important as your work appointments, because it is. Your dedication will help you become much more successful at work."

"I'm reminded again of my friend that sells insurance. Remember him? He spends time at the office every day interacting with clients. He gets the heavy lifting done, delegates his busy work to his assistant, and is home by three in the afternoon most days. He doesn't spend the day talking to co-workers or discussing his clients with other agents. He gets his work done and then he's gone.

He spends every minute of the workday doing something that makes him money. He delegates all remedial tasks to his assistant and dismisses distractions without another thought. He's usually there when his kids get home from school and he's able to spend valuable time with them. He certainly has other interests and hobbies, which he finds the time to do, but he has a balance. The scale doesn't lean to one side or the other. You have to find a way to balance your family, work, hobbies, interests, and service."

I knew Gage was right. I need to be able to be away from home to be successful and provide for my family. I can't leave my job before my work is finished.

However, I couldn't leave the Partition Project to someone else. I had always felt I had to be there and ensure everything was running smoothly.

"I can see the wheels spinning. What are you thinking?"

"I understand what you're saying, but how can spending less time at the office make me more successful?"

"I'm not saying to spend less time—I'm saying that you need to streamline your day so you're only spending your time doing the work that makes you money. To run at peak efficiency, you need to be delegating everything else. For example, do you have any idea how much of your time is wasted talking to time-killers?"

"Time-killers?" I was getting confused again.

"Yeah, you know—colleagues who show up in your office and talk about everything but the job. Like what happened over the weekend, what their kids are doing, or their most recent trip to Cancun."

"So what? People do that all the time."

"I know, and what they have to say is important to them. You need to be a good listener, but you also must have limits. Every minute you allow a time-killer to steal is a minute that you'll never get back."

"So are you suggesting I just ignore them?"

"Yes—I mean, without offending them of course. Think about it—your time is finite. You can't buy, borrow, or steal more. Every minute is precious. I know when I'm working at peak efficiency that I can get more done in just a few hours than a normal person can finish in an eight-hour day. How are you going to use your time?"

"Remind me what this has to do with balance?"

"I know this is hard to grasp, but believe me—it has everything to do with balance. Think about it, how do you spend your time? I use the word spend on purpose," Gage asked.

We had reached a section where the trail began to narrow. I followed him through thick trees that eventually led us onto a rocky cliff. Gage walked to the edge and looked to the other side. I had stopped, as I didn't want to get any closer to the edge. Gage turned and motioned for me to approach. I walked towards him reluctantly as I noticed the view was breathtaking, but the drop-off made my stomach curl. A narrow ridge spanned the vast expanse, connected to a cliff on the other side.

"Chance, what would you do if I told you that on the cliff over there is all the financial success you've ever dreamed of? If you can reach the other side you'll have more money than you know what to do with. Would you risk crossing it?"

I thought, there is no way I am going to cross that ridge. The path was sheer, falling almost vertically for hundreds of feet on both sides. One wrong step either way and it's over. I didn't reply, however, and I felt sweat beading up on my forehead. Gage could sense I was growing nervous.

"What's wrong? Did you hear my question?"

"Of course I did, but the ridge—I mean, there's no way I can possibly—"

"So you're scared?" Gage interrupted.

"Yes. Well, maybe more nervous—"

"What could possibly make you nervous? I just told you if you successfully cross to the other side all of your financial concerns disappear."

"I heard what you said—the operative word there is successfully. I don't know if I can successfully cross."

"Of course you can. Just take one step at a time."

The more I looked at it the more nervous I felt. Gage was acting indifferent—as if the possibility of falling wasn't a big deal.

Gage walked over to a ledge behind me.

"Chance, turn around." I obeyed and turned to see Gage leaning up against a large boulder. "Chance, this cliff represents the financial success you could have—all you need to do is cross. The ridge is just the road you have to follow—it will lead you to the success you desire."

"Road to success? It looks more like the death trap to success," I replied sarcastically.

Gage laughed, "I imagine it does to you. But do you think it can be safely crossed?"

"I'm sure a seasoned mountain climber could, or maybe someone who isn't afraid of heights."

"Okay Chance, I'll give you that. It looks risky, but isn't the road to success risky too?"

"Yes—and that's why most people don't reach it."

"I was talking about balance earlier today. The road to success must have balance or you could fall as easily as you could off either side of this cliff. And judging from the looks of the drop, that wouldn't feel good."

"I don't think I could balance myself across the ridge—I don't have that kind of physical balance," I stammered back.

"Very few people do, but that's not what I'm asking. If you focus all your efforts on your work, what you see behind you will be your road to success. Do you think success comes from hard work alone?"

"Probably not?"

"That sounded like a question."

"I'm not sure where you're going with this," I shot back defensively.

"Chance, I'll make it easy for you. What do you need to be successful?"

"Perseverance?"

"Good—anything else?"

"I have to decide what I want to do. I thought I had it all figured out with the Partition Project, but I know now that I need to find something else."

"Precisely, you need purpose—the ability to know what you need to focus on. When you focus, your purpose will become your passion.

If not, you'll wander aimlessly with no particular drive or direction. I'll use my insurance friend again as an example. He focuses on insurance, so what do you think he attracts?"

"Insurance sales."

"Exactly! The human mind really is a wonderful thing. We've already discussed this, but it's so important I thought it was worth mentioning again. When you are focused, your mind will program itself to attract what it needs in order for you to obtain what you are focused on."

"Well that's good, because I want a boat. I'll focus real hard and when I get home, the boat will be in my driveway right?" I thought I was being funny, but Gage wasn't laughing with me.

"You don't realize how close you are to the mark. I sense your sarcasm, but the principle is as real as the air we're breathing right now. The boat won't be in your driveway, but if that is your focus, your mind will come up with a way for you to obtain the funds to purchase the boat."

He was right. I thought back to when I was growing up. My cousins had just gotten a trampoline and after a visit to their house, my sisters and I begged my dad for one. There was nothing we wanted more than a trampoline.

My dad made us a deal. He told us we could have one if we saved half of the money that he would cover the other half. However, he said we could only use money that we'd earned through work—no allowance or birthday money.

We started the next day, but since we were too young to get jobs, we had to be resourceful. I considered mowing lawns for the neighbors, but everyone already had a lawn care service or kids of their own to do it.

Mom decided to help us out, showing us how to make potholders out of yarn and went with us to sell them around the neighborhood.

We knocked on every door in the neighborhood, and the majority of our neighbors purchased one or more of our potholders. We counted our money to see how close we were to our goal. We had to raise $250 and we were about $200 short. After all of the time we had invested into making the potholders and soliciting the neighbors—and all we had to show for it was fifty dollars. We were discouraged, but we weren't about to give up—we decided to take things to the next level.

We made cookies for my dad to take to work. He put the box out on the sales counter—each cookie was twenty-five cents. We made dozens of them, with mom's help, of course. They sold well, but after a few weeks we were still well short of our goal. Realizing this, we tried to figure out something else to earn that trampoline.

So mom taught us how to make lollipops. We made our first batch and we voila—we were in the lollipop business. Again, we hit the neighborhood door to door, and dad also took some to work again. We sold so many lollipops that we thought we would finally hit that $250 mark. Even though they sold like crazy, it still wasn't enough.

By now, summer was half over. We were all discouraged and almost to the point of giving up. Dad thought we'd come too far to quit—although he was proud of what we had done so far, he also wasn't going to just give in and buy it for us. He had made the deal with the intent that we would earn every cent of our half of the money.

I tried on more than one occasion to get him to call it good and just let us off the hook. He wouldn't budge, but he did do something else. He went to the store and purchased the trampoline. He placed it in pieces in the garage. Every day, we had to walk into the garage at some point, and there sat our trampoline in pieces. Some people might think this was cruel, but was the motivation we needed in order to reach our goal.

Again, with mom's help, we came up with one final idea that was certain to put us over the top—tissue box holders. We made them out of a plastic latticework and yarn. We were so close, just fifty dollars away from our trampoline! We set out on the streets for what would be our last tour of the neighborhood. By now, pretty much all of our neighbors knew exactly who we were and what we were after. Many opened the doors and rolled their eyes—I think mom was getting embarrassed with how we solicited our neighbors, but we were learning a great lesson and our parents understood that. As we were making our rounds one afternoon, we'd made it around the block and sales were good. We had three houses and twenty-five dollars to go. We knocked on a door and were greeted by our neighbor who had purchased from us before.

"Oh man! Not you kids again. Don't you have that trampoline yet?"

"No sir, but we're close—we're hoping to have it this week."

"How much have you earned so far?" he asked us.

"Two hundred and twenty-five dollars," we chimed back in unison. We were proud of that amount too. Raising the money we needed had been harder than we'd ever anticipated.

"How much do you need to put you over the top?"

"Twenty-five dollars," we answered.

Our neighbor reached into his pocket, pulling out his wallet. He picked out two bills, a twenty and a five. He handed them to us, smiling as he asked, "Will this do it?"

"YES SIR! Thank you so much!" we chimed back, barely able to contain our excitement.

"Good, now I don't want to see you selling stuff at my door anymore. Oh and by the way, my kids want to come over and jump on your trampoline. Would you or your parents give us a ring when you get it set up?"

We told him yes, and with that he shut the door. We took off, running for home as fast as we could. We had reached our goal and we were excited to show our parents. I still remember all the times where we wanted to give up but didn't. We hung in there and we finally earned the money. We could hardly wait for dad to get home. By the time he walked through the door we had organized the pile of money into neatly organized stacks. He counted the money and smiled, "Let's set up your trampoline." That trampoline was our focus and, along with mom's help, we eventually came up with a way to reach that goal.

As I reflected on my childhood, I suddenly started to understand what Gage was trying to teach me. I thought over the trampoline experience again, recalling how focused my sisters and I were on reaching our goal.

We reached it without letting our chores suffer and we still did the usual family things we had always done. We had found additional time to spend on our project—and we did it as a family and as I looked back I could still remember how much fun we'd had. I was starting to grasp what he was trying to say about balance.

"Gage, I apologize for the sarcasm, but I'm starting to see what you're saying," I told him as I recounted my story about the trampoline and what I learned from the experience to him.

"Chance, that's exactly what I'm talking about—you brought a balanced approach to your project and you and your sisters succeeded in more ways than one.

Not only did you achieve your goal, but it sounds like you learned a lot about life from the experience as well." Gage glanced behind me and smiled, "Turn around Chance—look at your ridge top."

I turned around to look. To my astonishment the trail had grown considerably wider. In fact, it almost looked passable. I was still nervous about the drop-off on each side, but now I thought I could cross safely.

"Chance, the road to your goals is much easier if you have balance. I have something else I want to talk to you about." I turned and looked at Gage as he continued, "Chance, don't underestimate the importance of family support. Most of all, you need the support of your wife. Our challenges and setbacks are much easier to overcome with the support of the ones we love. Kelsea and your daughters deserve much more of your time— you need to be there for them more. I promise, if you're there for them they'll be there for you also."

"You're right," I replied. "Kelsea has been a huge support through this—in fact, her support has made things much easier."

With that realization I looked back toward the trail. It was definitely wide enough—the fear of falling quickly evaporated.

"Chance, if you have balance in your life the path to success will be easier to pass and seem much more obtainable. Your goals will have more meaning once you achieve them. However, if your mind is narrow, you run the risk of falling off one side or the other. When your mind is open and balanced, falling off is much more difficult—if not totally impossible."

CHAPTER 12

Trust in the Outcome

The sun hung low in the sky as we returned to Elephant Rock. I'd learned a lot about committing myself to balancing my life. My mindset was different now than prior to my termination—Gage really was teaching me to think in new ways.

"Chance, I want you to come back tomorrow, but there's something I want you to do tonight."

"Anything, you name it."

"I want to give you another assignment that will pull you from your comfort zone. I guess I want to place you in an uncomfortable position so I can see how you handle it."

"You already sent me to your funeral, wasn't that hard enough?"

"I admit that the funeral was hard, but we already discussed that. This will make you even more uncomfortable, but I have confidence in you."

"What could possibly be more difficult than going to your funeral?"

"I want you to go home and tell Kelsea about our meetings. I want you to tell her you've speaking with me."

I sat in silent disbelief for a moment. Gage was right—this was going to be way more difficult than Gage's funeral. Honestly, I didn't want to do it. "No way! She'll think I'm crazy. I'm not going to tell her."

"Yes you are, and once you explain things she'll be fine with it. You tell her I'm training you to take over my position running Kempton Motors."

My heart leapt at Gage's statement—could it be true? Was he really training me to take his place? What a flattering thought!

I suddenly knew what I wanted. The goal and how to accomplish it suddenly appeared to me. I felt a surge of excitement hit me. My smile must have given away my feelings.

"You like that idea—don't you?"

"It sounds great! But why me?"

"You're the only one that can see me—you were the only one that came up the trail that day."

"But what about Donald?"

"Donald can't run my company, he's not you. It's going to take time, but Don will see it too. He's a smart guy, but he knows he can't run the company long-term and he doesn't want to. If he wanted the job, he would've taken it when I offered it to him several years ago. I wanted him to run the company so I could step down and enjoy the world."

"I don't know what to say."

"Don't say anything. Talk to Kelsea—tell her what's going on. See if she'll support you.
That is, if you want the job."

"Of course I want it. Thank you, I can't tell you how much it means to even have the opportunity— it's unbelievable!"

"You'll do just fine, I'm sure of it. Remember though—you're a product of what you set your mind to. That's it Chance. It's time for you to go home and discuss the last few days with Kelsea. See how it goes."

I asked myself, what do I have to lose by telling Kelsea? She won't overreact—at least I didn't think she would.

She'd been amazing so far through this whole ordeal, but then again there was no way to tell for sure how she would react when she heard I'd been learning about success from a dead man. I quickly dismissed the negative thoughts and focused on only positives—telling myself over and over that she'd be okay with everything. Oh well, I was willing to give anything a shot for the opportunity to one day have Gage's job.

I waved goodbye to Gage and started making my way back down the trail. By the time I got to my car it was almost completely dark. I hardly noticed, however, my mind was racing as I tried to formulate the right words to tell Kelsea about Gage. My fear was mainly with her reaction. Nonetheless, I hoped she trusted me enough not to have me committed on the spot. I pulled into our garage in no time at all and nervously walked into the house. Kelsea was in the kitchen putting away dishes—looks like I'd missed another dinner.

"Hey, we were expecting you for dinner," Kelsea said. She was so irritated she dropped the dishes she had been holding and they loudly clanged into the sink.

I immediately felt guilty. It was late and it was obvious she could have used my help getting dinner prepared.

"Where are the girls?"

"In bed! Where else? They went down an hour ago."

"I'll go check on them."

"No, don't. They were restless and I don't want you to wake them up. You'll see them in the morning."

She was irritated and understandably so. My concern was in her current state of mind my story may be even more difficult to digest. I wanted to put off talking to her but I was heading back to see Gage in the morning. There wasn't much time before my interview with Donald.

"Kelsea—umm—well, there's something I need to tell you."

Kelsea's mouth dropped, her eyes widened with the anticipation of receiving bad news.

"What Chance? What is it?"

"It's just—I want to tell you what I've actually been doing the past few days."

Kelsea put her hand over her mouth, tears started streaming down her cheeks. I didn't know why she was upset.

"Tell me Chance—tell me now. No, don't tell me—I don't want to know. Wait, no, tell me, before I change my mind," she said through clenched teeth as anger filled her voice.

I didn't understand why she was acting like this. But then I thought of what had just transpired. She was thinking the worst.

"Honey, it's nothing bad," her strange behavior was making me uncomfortable.

"I'll be the judge of that," Kelsea snapped.

"I just want to tell you who I've been meeting on my hikes."

"Stop Chance! Just tell me her name. I understand you've been under a lot of pressure we can make it through this but I want her name."

An affair? She thought I was seeing another woman? That had never even occurred to me. "Gage—is the person's name that I've been meeting," I said quickly.

"Gage? That's a funny name for a woman."

"Gage isn't a woman. He's a he. In fact, you know who he is."

Her enraged expressed changed to total confusion. "A guy? Is Gage a friend I've never met?"

"Gage Kempton. I've been meeting him on my hikes to Elephant Rock."

"Gage Kempton? How can that be true? He died a few days ago!"

"He did, but I've been meeting with him. The day after I was fired I hiked to Elephant Rock and there he was—only at the time I didn't know he was dead.

He told me to come back the next day, but warned me that I'd hear something about him on the news.

He made me promise to return regardless. That was the day you told me he was killed. Obviously I didn't tell you because you would've thought I was crazy. I'm telling you now because—"

"Because he asked you to?" Kelsea's question interrupted me mid-sentence.

"Yes—but how?" I trailed off as Kelsea turned and walked over to her laptop, motioning me to follow. She pulled up her email account and highlighted a message she'd received. She stood to the side so I could read it.

I just wanted to see if he would do it.

GK

"I had no idea what this meant—I almost erased it, but it makes sense now. Look at the email address it was sent from."

I looked at the screen and read:

gk@kempton.motors.com

"I can't believe this," I said in total disbelief.

"He must've known I would think you're going crazy—I still do a bit," she said smiling back at me finally. "I'd rather you were meeting with a ghost than another woman."

"You know I'd never do that to you."

"I know, but you weren't doing a very good job at explaining yourself," Kelsea joked as she was finally appearing to relax.

"Yeah, my bad," I chuckled back.

"So, what is he telling you?"

"He didn't reveal what he wants from me until today," I said as I began relating my experiences on Elephant Rock to her, giving her every single detail that I could remember. She was intrigued by what I said, but the best part was she actually believed me—as crazy as I sounded.

"I don't know why this is happening to me, but it is."

"It's happening to you because you're a wonderful, talented person. I can see that in you, and I can definitely see you as the president of Kempton Motors."

It felt good to hear Kelsea say that. I needed the confidence boost that only she could give me. "Are you going back tomorrow?"

"Yes, but I have a feeling he is almost done with me. He's ready to continue on. I think he just wants to make sure I'm ready for my interview with Donald."

"Good luck, and please tell him I received his email."

"Oh don't worry—I'll mention that for sure."

CHAPTER 13

Navigating Roadblocks

I drove my car toward the canyon. Up ahead I noticed orange barrels blocking the road with a large sign that read, Road closed, and pointing toward a detour to the right.

"Great!" I said. Now it was going to take twice as long to get to the trailhead. I followed one detour sign after another. I wound through neighborhoods I didn't recognize. Eventually, it led me back to the main road. I drove up the canyon and pulled into my usual parking spot. I was running about ten minutes behind due to the detour.

I smiled as I saw Gage waiting for me as I approached Elephant Rock. "You did as I asked," Gage said.

"How'd you know?"

"I got a message from Kelsea last night thanking me for the warning."

"You warned her and let me sweat it out."

"I wanted to make sure you would show up today. I know how women think. If she thought you were crazy, or worse, she would have never let you come back."

"Good call—at first she thought I was having an affair." Gage started laughing hysterically. "I'm glad you find this so funny," I told him sarcastically.

When he had finally calmed down enough to speak he shot me a sly glance, "Well, we can't have that now, can we?"

"No, we can't."

"You weren't going to tell her. I'm proud of you."

"Well thanks—it was hard."

"Stepping outside your comfort zone is never easy, but once you do, it gets easier and easier. It's a necessity in business, and in life for that matter. You won't grow unless you take a step outside the box every once in a while."

"I guess I understand. There were several things we did on the Partition Project that were out of the standard protocol for networking systems but ended up being a crucial part of the Project's success. I guess you could say we 'stepped outside the box' in a manner of speaking," I replied thoughtfully.

"I remember when Don wanted to bring on Mini. The car was too small and there was only one model with any options—talk about stepping outside the box! It felt like a huge risk at the time, but it ended up being a huge success. Our Mini sales climbed every year, eventually becoming one of our top sellers. You see Chance? Stepping out of your comfort zone is very important. I look at my insurance agent friend—he had to step out of his zone every morning when he picked up the phone. He did it until it became comfortable. He attributes his phoning skills to his enormous success. Remember—on a regular basis successful people do the things that unsuccessful people are not willing to do. Stepping outside your comfort zone is a big part of that."

I knew Gage was right. I thought of most people who are satisfied punching the clock every day, doing the things they are comfortable with—never putting themselves out there.

Gage made perfect sense. I guess my mind had been closed off when it should have been open. I thought about it for a moment—I had felt the need to shift gears plenty of times in my career.

It wasn't always my choice, but that doesn't mean I couldn't be successful doing something else. Gage was definitely right. My entire mindset was changing. I was reevaluating everything I'd ever thought or believed in. I felt confident that if I focused I could be successful doing anything.

Successful people learn to adjust and deal with whatever is thrown their way. I thought back to the roadblock on my way to the trail today. I wondered how many times in my life I had encountered one and quit or stopped completely instead of taking a detour? I guess every roadblock is accompanied by a detour—we just have to look for the sign. There'll always be roadblocks on the road to success, but I was realizing I just had to look until I found a way around it. The road may take me through unfamiliar territory, but perseverance will get me back on the road and to the final destination.

CHAPTER 14

Taking New Direction

Kelsea greeted me at the door. It was nice she was aware of my meetings with Gage. I didn't like feeling like I was going behind her back or that I wasn't being completely honest with her.

"How did things go with Gage today?" she asked sweetly.

"Really well, and he thinks I'm ready for my meeting with Donald.

"That's good, isn't it?"

"Of course it is, but I'm still nervous. "

"I'm sure you'll do fine, especially if Gage thinks you're ready."

"I hope you're right, but I can't let on I've been talking to Gage or Donald will think I'm crazy."

"I know the feeling Chance, believe me. Just be yourself—you can't go wrong. You have all the knowledge you need to ace the interview. The things Gage has taught you will take you to the top."

"I appreciate your vote of confidence."

"Chance, I have all the confidence in the world in you because I know what you're capable of. You're a huge success, especially to me."

I loved hearing Kelsea say that. There was something I wanted to make clear right now. "Kelsea, I'm sorry for all the times I haven't been there—I'm sorry for working all those late nights, especially when you were counting on me to be here and I wasn't around."

"Chance, stop. I understand you need to work—its fine, I get it. I'm sure as you progress with Kempton you'll be needed more and more," Kelsea reassured me.

"No, it's not fine. I'm committing to you right now I'll be there," I told her. "I'll give my work nine hours a day but the rest is yours. There may be times I have to work more than that, but when that happens I promise to make it up to you. From here on out our family comes first. I won't miss anything the girls do. I'll be there for them and for you."

Kelsea seemed pleasantly surprised—her eyes were starting to tear up again. I gathered her up in my arms, giving her a huge hug.

"I like this new Chance," she said as she looked up into my eyes. I was starting to like the new Chance too.

CHAPTER 15

Living in Gratitude

Gage sat waiting for me on top of Elephant Rock. As I approached, he stood and waved. "Good morning," I said as I neared his position.

"Chance come up here and sit down. We're going to take it easy today. I want to talk to you about something that is very important."

"I thought everything you talk about is important."

"Well of course, but today's topic is something that is becoming extinct in today's modern world. In fact, this principle is probably more important today than ever before. Can you guess what I'm talking about?"

"Not a clue, Gage."

"Gratitude—I want to talk to you about gratitude," Gage responded.

"Gratitude? You mean like being thankful?" I asked.

"That's exactly what I'm talking about. We live in a world that is missing the point. We are spoiled, and we have to have everything right now. Computer companies work feverishly to make their products faster and more efficient. Internet speeds constantly increase.

We have cable and satellite television broadcasting whatever we want twenty four hours a day.

No one saves money for big expenses anymore. You don't buy a car, you partner with the bank and use their car. As long as you make the payment, they let you park it in your garage. The same goes for many things. I went to a store not too long ago to purchase a computer monitor and they asked me if I was interested in their payment plan!"

"Didn't you build an empire on people making payments?"

"Of course I did. But that doesn't change the facts. As a society we have become selfish. There was a time when neighbors watched out for each other, but those days are a fading memory. Everything is me, me, me and I, I, I. Just watch the evening news—how many athletes give the credit to their teams for the win? Not many, but I see more and more that discuss what they did for the win—it's almost like they were playing the game by themselves. Sure, there are still great athletes, but they seem to be getting harder and harder to find as well. Showing gratitude is a must if our society expects to survive. We need to be grateful for what we have and the opportunities we are given. It seems the only time we think of others is during the holidays. I fear for our society if this doesn't stop. Remember, we are what we send out. If we are sending out gratitude, we will all prosper. Tell the people you love how thankful you are for them and be grateful for the people who work for you—they are an integral part of your success.

Give them your gratitude and I promise they will work that much harder. Show your gratitude through service—I told you about the kids in the hospital and their families that we help. But on a much smaller scale, showing gratitude can be as simple as shoveling the walks of an elderly neighbor or volunteering at the local homeless shelter or food bank. Showing gratitude is as simple as sending a card to someone you love and expressing how thankful you are for them."

I thought about what Gage was saying. I was very thankful for my family, but I didn't usually take the time to show anyone else gratitude.

"My grandmother was a great example of someone who showed gratitude every day. She loved everyone around her— including those who some people shun. She served several meals for people in need and she always enjoyed having people for dinner. She loved cooking for anyone. She also made hundreds of blankets for needy children all over the world. She did this until well into her nineties. Even when she began going blind in both eyes it didn't stop her—she just kept on going. Her motto was if you can't have what you want, like what you have—she lived by that."

"She sent out gratitude to others and that was exactly what she got back. In return, people loved to help her when she was in need. When she was too weak to climb the stairs to her second story apartment, a friend gave up his ground floor apartment for her."

"She spent her final few years in an assisted living center— all of the staff and residents took an instant liking to her of course. Her magnetic personality and attitude of gratitude attracted many new friends. She didn't have much as far as worldly possessions are concerned, but she had enduring friendships she paid it forward, backwards and all around. She always took the lead in serving and showing gratitude to those around her."

I thought of those people in need around me. The past few years I'd been too busy with my career and immediate family. I hadn't even visited my own grandmother in months.

"Chance, what are you thinking about?"

"I'm thinking of the improvements I need to make when it comes to gratitude. I need to pay closer attention to those in need."

"Your life will be blessed if you follow this principle. You'll find new ways to succeed and doors will open for you. I know it sounds simple, and it is—you just need to do it."

Once again Gage had put my mind in motion. I'd learned a lot, but today was the first time I had felt guilty for the things I wasn't doing. I felt ashamed I hadn't been trying to show anyone that I was grateful for them.

"I know what you're thinking Chance. Don't worry about the past. What's done is done. Start now, start today, all is not lost. Just pay attention and watch for opportunities."

"I will. I understand the principle and I will."

"Good. Will you be back tomorrow?"

"I will. Only one more day before my interview."

"And you are prepared. Tomorrow I want to discuss one last thing, but I'm confident you're ready," Gage said, giving me a wink.

CHAPTER 16

Lessons from Unlikely Sources

The morning air was crisp. It had cooled considerably from the night before due to a cold front that had passed through. The temperature was perfect for a hike—not too hot but not too cold. I didn't even break a sweat on the switchbacks. As I approached the rock I saw Gage, but he didn't seem to notice me or give his usual wave. He appeared fixated by something on the rock.

"Good morning?" I said attempting to get his attention.

"Ants are amazing creatures, aren't they?" Gage didn't look up, his gaze still fixated on the rock.

"Ants? What the heck are you talking about?"

"Come up here and look," he said. As I got closer, I saw that he was staring at a small group of ants on the rock just a few feet in front of him.

I pulled myself up to Gage's position and looked down and focused on the spot he was studying. I saw a line of ants, most carrying small leaves as they walked across the rock. I wondered why Gage found this so intriguing. Maybe now that he's dead he has the time to notice the small things.

"Gage, I've gotta be honest here—I don't get it."

"These ants are carrying more than fifty times their body weight."

"So?"

"So? How much do you weigh?"

"One seventy-five," I said as I puffed out my chest proudly.

"Could you carry an item that weighs over 8,750 pounds?"

"Of course not!"

"Tell me then, why can this creature carry that much weight?"

"I have no idea Gage."

"It's because no one has told it that it can't! There's a lesson here, and it's actually all around us. Nature is the master teacher. How often do you just sit and observe nature?"

"I'm in the mountains all the time, but I guess other than watching the occasional deer or sitting to take a drink and feel the wind in my face, I don't really observe."

"Start!" Gage said almost shouting. "There are many lessons to be learned."

Gage's time must have been getting close, I thought. He didn't seem to be making much sense any more. Or I couldn't grasp what he was trying to tell me. What could I possibly learn from nature? Yeah, it's pretty cool that ants can carry all that weight, but isn't that how they're designed.

"Chance, take a look at those squirrels over there. What are they doing?" Gage asked interrupting my thoughts.

I looked over to see two squirrels scampering about under a large pine tree. "Ummm, gathering nuts?"

"Exactly, they're gathering nuts. Why do you think they're gathering nuts?"

"Because they're hungry?" I asked stating what I thought was obvious.

"If they were hungry, wouldn't they be eating them?" Gage asked thoughtfully. "Listen Gage, I'm not following what you're getting at here. Are you okay?"

"Have I led you astray yet?" Gage asked with piercing eyes.

"No, of course not."

"Then indulge me for a moment, will you?" Gage asked, shaking his head.

"Okay then, I suppose it makes sense—they'd be eating the nuts if they were hungry."

"So what are they doing?"

"I still have no idea Gage."

"They're preparing."

"Preparing?"

"For winter! They gather nuts all summer so they can survive the winter. So what can we learn from the squirrels?"

I thought of all the things I wanted to say, but luckily they didn't make it past my brain's filter. "I don't know Gage, maybe they'll starve, who knows!"

"Despite your sarcasm, you're exactly right. At Kempton Motors we bank on dry spells every year. I had a good idea of when they would occur, but timing the duration was sometimes a challenge.

My team had to account for the slow times by saving money during the good times. I guess you could say we saved our nuts."

Okay, that's funny, I thought as I chuckled to myself. I knew now where he was trying to go with this. I thought Gage's methods were strange, but I knew the lesson he wanted me to learn. We'd had the same issues and I thought lack of preparation might have actually been a big factor in my termination. If the company had planned better and prepared for bad times, my job may have been spared.

"So what else has nature taught you?" The sarcasm left my voice—I was genuinely interested in what Gage had to say.

"Spiders, I hate spiders. I hate spiders worse than anything. It doesn't matter if the spider is big or small, I can't deal with them. If I saw a spider on the wall in our home I made my wife get it."

"You're a brave man Gage."

"I know it sounds crazy, but there's something to learn from spiders also. Spiders are opportunists. They spin their webs and wait.

They spend their entire life waiting for unsuspecting prey to stick to their web. Once the insect is stuck, the spider springs into action, immobilizing it with poison. Eventually, the arachnid feeds on its prize—doing nothing other than spinning an intricate net. Do you need more? Can you see the lesson?"

"Yeah, stay away from spider webs."

"Have you ever walked into a spider's web?"

"Of course I have."

"Did you see it coming?"

"No, otherwise I would have ducked or walked around."

"Exactly! Never allow yourself to be the unsuspecting victim. Know your colleagues, get to know and understand your customer. Visit your competitors—shake their hands, develop relationships with them. Anyone can spin a web—you won't be able to see it until it's too late. Watch out for it— recognize the web before it is even spun. Don't let anyone undermine your goals, and most of all don't let anyone squash your dreams"

As I was allowing that lesson to sink into my mind, Gage went on. "Look at the trees."

"The trees?"

"Trees are a miracle—they do something seemingly impossible."

"And what's that?"

"Trees defy gravity. Every tree starts as a small seed and keeps pushing higher and higher towards the sky. They stand in defiance of gravity. And what is the lesson?"

"Keep pushing upward, don't quit."

"You're getting good at this. What about snakes?"

"I hate snakes as much as you hate spiders."

"Why do you hate snakes?"

"Because they bite."

"Are you speaking from personal experience?"

"Actually I am. When I was young, there was a river that ran through the back of my grandparent's property. I was there with a friend and he dared me to pick up a snake. At the time I loved snakes. They had beautiful markings I found fascinating. I gladly picked up the snake, but the second I did it turned its head and bit me. Luckily it wasn't poisonous."

"So you were bitten just once?"

"Yes, once."

"And you never picked up a snake again, no matter how fascinating it looked."

"Yeah, and I never will."

"See? You learned your lesson. Do you see my point?"

"Don't pick up snakes." I said hesitantly

"You'll meet people who seem wonderful. I guarantee a friend or someone you trust will eventually bite you. You will have business deals that seem foolproof, but you will end up losing a lot of money. I believe in risk and trusting others, but once something or someone betrays that trust it's over. And if I get bitten, I won't pick up a snake again," Gage looked at me for a minute before he continued. "Do you recognize snakes?"

"Yes, they're not hard to miss."

"Once you're bitten by a snake they become even harder to miss. This also goes for people. You only have to be bitten once before you start to recognize the snakes. My son loves chameleons. He has two of them in an aquarium in his bedroom. Very interesting creatures with unique features. They are difficult to describe because they are a reptile, but don't look like a normal lizard. They're one of a kind. What ability does a chameleon have that most other reptiles lack?"

"I know their skin can change color?" I said, my answer more of a question than an answer.

"Yes, they blend into their surroundings."

"Okay, so that's kind of cool—"

"But what is the lesson?" Gage's question cut me short.

"Try to blend in?"

"They are unique— they don't look like any other reptile. They don't just have subtle differences— they have major ones. All they do is blend in. Do you know how many people I know who're like that? They are different and talented in many ways— they have the potential to be great. But all they want to do is blend in, to not be noticed. They think by blending in they camouflage themselves, hiding from disappointment and rejection. However, what they're really doing is holding themselves back from growth and eliminating their potential to succeed."

As I was about to reply to Gage I caught sight of some movement in the trees. We sat in silence. Something was there— we heard the snap of the occasional branch and leaves rustling. The animal decided to make an appearance. A large moose stepped out of the bushes and onto the trail just a few yards from us and was closely followed by a young calf.

Gage smiled at me. "Here's another lesson in nature. I'm not going to demonstrate, but that moose will do anything to protect her calf. She'll attack if she feels even the slightest threat of danger. The odds are against you with a charging moose protecting her young."

Gage didn't have to say anything else. I understood the lesson completely. We watched as the moose slowly wandered off into the woods, back up the slope toward the ridge.

"I look at nature and know there's a God. I asked you a few days ago if you prayed. I don't care what the answer is, but if you don't, you should. We can only get so far on our own in life. We need divine guidance to show us the way. I can't tell you how many times I've hit snags in my life, but through prayer things have seemed to work out.

Balance Chance, everything has must have a balance. Prayer has been a part of mine. I have found if I humble myself, and prayerfully set goals, they become much easier to accomplish. I felt as if I had a partner upstairs helping me out. I really don't care if you're religious or not. You can believe in a grand creator and never step foot in a church."

"So you feel nature proves to you the existence of a God."

Gage looked at me, and his face seemed to glow. "Don't you find it interesting that the governing body of this earth, the source of warmth and light is called the sun?"

As Gage looked at me, his face started glowing brighter than I had seen it. I've never thought that deeply before. I've never thought to look to nature for anything but recreation and beauty. I've never considered these things, but they all made such perfect sense. Gage was suggesting I become observant of my surroundings and learn from everything I see. I could feel it was true—like every lesson I'd learned from him. He allowed me to experience everything he taught. Today as no different—in fact, I think I felt more alive today than at any other time in my life.

"I think Don will be impressed. I think he'll even hire you on the spot. He'd be crazy not to." Gage paused as a tear down his cheek. I wondered what was wrong. I wasn't sure if he was happy or sad. I hoped I hadn't done anything to upset him.

"Is everything okay Gage?"

"Couldn't be better—you've grown a lot Chance. Just remember what we talked about."

I suddenly knew why he was crying. This was going to be our last moment together. I didn't want him to go. I wanted him to stay here forever. I wanted to be able to bounce ideas off him whenever I wanted. I felt comfortable knowing he was there.

"Can't you at least wait until after my meeting?"

"I'm done here Chance. You're ready. I'm proud of you. I don't know for certain what the outcome of the meeting will be, but I am already proud of you."

"Will you come back?"

"I don't know Chance." Gage seemed unsure as he looked towards the sky and smiled. "I'll be here when you need me."

I felt good. I was so glad I hiked the trail the day I was fired instead of going golfing. I learned so much more than I'd ever imagined.

"You better head down Chance. It's getting late."

A few hours of daylight still remained, but I caught the hint. He needed to get going more than me. I looked at Gage—he gave me that wave I had become accustomed to for the last few days.

I waved back and started down the trail. After a few feet I turned and looked back. He was gone—the space he had occupied on the rock was empty. But I knew I would always be grateful for the space he filled within me.

My throat started feeling tense and dry as tears started streaming down my cheeks. I wasn't sure if I was sad to see Gage leave or happiness for the new outlook on life Gage had given me. I felt a confidence that I'd never felt before—I knew that I could overcome my fears and accomplish whatever goals I set my mind to. I knew I would never forget the lessons he taught or the manner in which he taught them. Gage knew what I needed, but rather than just telling me, he showed me, using the washed out trail and its downed tree, the mud on my boots, and Nicholas' prosthetic leg. He sent me to his funeral with two tasks—both of which I accomplished, even though they caused me anxiety and discomfort.

He spoke of friends and acquaintances who have been successful, but who had also suffered unnecessary sacrifices in their quest for success. And then there was the mountain lion, where I was forced to face my ultimate fear of death. I learned no matter how tired and worn out I was, whether mentally or physically, with proper motivation I would always have more to give. Gage taught me the importance of balance—he led me to a narrow ridge that seemed impossible, which widened as he showed me what a balanced approach could do for my life.

He asked me to be honest with Kelsea by telling her where I was going each day. I'd always remember his lessons of nature— not just to pay more attention to my environment, but to also learn to apply what I see to my life.

Gage taught me the importance of giving back and about the law of attraction, especially how important it is to know and understand this governing law. He spoke of gratitude and what a better world we would live in if people could grasp on to the concept of being grateful to others and be grateful for what they have. He gave much of his time and resources for the benefit of others. Without Gage, people who needed help would have never gotten it. Most importantly, he became my mentor and friend. I hoped he would make another appearance someday.

I was excited about my appointment with Donald. Gage had prepared me well. What had started as a feeling that everything would be okay had turned into absolute knowledge—I knew everything would be okay. There wasn't a doubt in my mind.

EPILOGUE

Answering a Cry for Help

As I approached the bottom of the trail my thoughts reflected on the lessons I had learned from Gage over the past week. I missed him already and wished he hadn't had to go. I had a renewed confidence, not only in myself but in my abilities as well. I reached the final stretch and noticed a small gathering of people in the large meadow below me. A man and a young boy approached me on the trail.

"What's going on down there?" I asked, assuming they were with the group.

"Looks like a group camping trip to me," the man said as they continued up the trail, disappearing out of sight. I turned to see five kids coming up the trail, and recognized our neighbor Lizzy Jenson.

"What are you kids doing up here?" I asked.

"We're going for a hike," Lizzy said.

"Where are your parents?"

"They're setting up our tents—the whole neighborhood's here!" she said.

Something clicked in my mind. Every year our neighborhood has a camp-out on Rudy's flat in conjunction with the local church. I couldn't believe it was this weekend.

"You kids be careful, okay?"

They all nodded in agreement. I felt something strange, but quickly disregarded the feeling as my thoughts rested with Kelsea. I couldn't wait to tell her about my final day with Gage. I had a renewed commitment to Kelsea and my daughters. I didn't think it was possible to love them any more than I already did, but for some reason I felt closer to them.

As I approached the creek my daughters came running across the bridge towards me. Kelsea followed, walking behind them as they ran into my arms. I scooped them both up, excited to see them. What a wonderful surprise, I thought. "I'm guessing you came up with the others?" I asked Kelsea.

"I knew you didn't hear me yesterday when I told you we were coming. But that's okay. I thought we would get here early and wait for you to come down the trail."

I knew we had a camp-out this time of year, but she was right—I didn't remember Kelsea saying anything about it yesterday. My mind had been focused on Gage and our lessons like a laser. I felt bad, but I hadn't paid attention to much else.

"I don't have anything packed."

Kelsea smiled. "I packed for you. I think you'll survive for one night."

Camping wouldn't have been my first choice for tonight. I thought I'd rather sit at home and meditate for my upcoming appointment at Kempton Motors, but the more I thought about camping with my family the more I warmed up to it. It'd be a great opportunity to spend some quality time with Kelsea and the girls.

"Great! Do we need to set up a tent?"

"It's already done. We've been up here for an hour—I set up the tent in the old volleyball court. I figured that was a good spot where we wouldn't have to worry about laying on rocks all night." Camping and I don't have to set up? This was sounding better and better.

"Great! You lead the way." I followed Kelsea up the road for about two hundred yards to an area known as Rudy's Flat.

There was noise all around—I could hear people pounding in tent stakes, the clatter of pots and pans, screaming children, and people laughing and generally having a good time. Everyone was engaged in some type of an activity or another—I noticed a game of horseshoes going on next to a group setting up camp stoves.

"Girls, come here," I said kneeling down and motioning to them.

"I want both of you to have fun, but it can be dangerous up here. Don't wander off on your own. Promise me you'll stay close to me or mom, okay?" Both of my girls nodded back before getting up to follow Kelsea into the tent.

"Chance," I heard someone calling my name—I turned to see Spencer Malone and his son Robert just a few feet away unloading the back of a truck.

"Chance, can you give us a hand?" he asked politely. I gladly walked over to help and noticed they were trying to unload a large propane camp stove. The frame was heavy and awkward—I reached out to grab it but stopped as I heard a concerning noise. It almost sounded like a wounded animal, but I wasn't sure.

"Did you hear that?" I asked Spencer.

"Are you kidding me? Hear what? With all the commotion around here you're going to have to be a little more specific," Spencer said laughing as Robert shook his head.

I heard the subtle scream again and realized it was a distant call for help. I dropped my side of the stove and ran toward the direction the sound, my eyes scanning up the mountain. I could see objects through the trees, toward the side of the canyon with a sizeable cliff. The cliff had been formed by a landslide in the canyon several years back, which created such treacherous chutes that even the most experienced climber would avoid this unpredictable area filled with loose, slippery rocks.

As I cleared the trees, the scene before me almost stopped my heart. Two fluorescent shirts were clearly visible on the side of the cliff. I could see they were five young kids all in a panic, trying to make their way down the chute and headed straight toward the cliff. Instantly I knew they were the kids I had passed on the trail. I looked farther up the mountain.

The father and son I had passed appeared to be in need of help as well.

The young kids must have followed him out onto the slide and had gotten too far down and couldn't get back up. They had passed the point of no return—from where they were there was no way they were going to be able to get down on their own. I caught movement out of the corner of my eye and I turned to look just as a softball sized rock cut loose, tumbled down the hill, and hit one of the kids square in the head. A boy above him had kicked the rock free and was in danger of knocking more rocks loose.

I looked up to see the father and his son at the top of the slope. The man was trying to maneuver himself, but inadvertently sent a small boulder free. It struck a different boy directly above the other two who was already struggling to keep hold of the rocky slope. He lost his balance and by some miracle he was able to stay on his feet, holding his position by anchoring his butt squarely against the rock wall behind him. The kids were trying to get down, but each time they moved they were setting loose a steady stream of rock that was raining down on everyone below. To make things worse, they appeared to have no idea they were heading for a cliff. I watched the father and son as they managed to struggle their way safely back to the top.

By this time, Kelsea had joined me and she gasped, horrified at the scene before her. It looked grim. There were now four kids scattered along the rock face.

They were quickly approaching the cliff and they were so far down I knew they had no chance of making it back on their own.

"You have to save them," Kelsea told me. I knew she was right, but there was no way I could just run up there without creating more of a hazard for them and myself.

"Hang on, let me figure this out." I spoke with confidence.

Just then the boy at the top kicked another softball size rock onto the kid below him. Instinct kicked in once again.

"STOP! EVERYONE, STOP MOVING!" My voice carried far and they must have all heard me because instantly the kids stopped moving. The steep terrain created an awkward stance for the kids. Their butts were basically hitting the back of the rocky cliff and standing still for a long period of time was probably impossible. But if they could keep still for now, the rocks would stop falling and it would buy me a few minutes to get up there. I started running up the apron of loose shale as I thought there was no way I would be able to save these kids on my own.

I thought back to Gage's advice earlier that day—it seemed like forever ago—as I looked up and whispered, "Lord, I'm going to need your help on this one." As I muttered these words I felt an unexplainable strength hit my body and adrenaline filled my veins. My hands and feet worked quickly—I found each handhold and foothold with unprecedented ease as I climbed up the side of the cliff. My heart was pounding with fear, which I quickly dismissed. I couldn't allow fear to stop me from reaching the kids. A wrong move would mean serious injury or even certain death for all of us.

I reached the first child, it was our neighbor Lizzy Jenson. She had tears running down her dirty face and was whimpering in pain as I reached her.

"Hi honey, how are you?" Lizzy didn't respond, her eyes glazed over in agony. She stared straight into the distance as her young brain tried to cope with her terror.

Her skin was flushed—my first thought was she had slipped into shock. I realized I had to move even more quickly, if they were in shock time was even more critical.

"I'm going to grab your arm, I promise I won't let go, but you'll have to slide down on your butt— your butt's your friend on this one," I said, trying to sound calm. I turned to look back and evaluate my position, unsure of how exactly I was going to get down if I was going to have to hold her. I quickly pointed out the hand and footholds I had used to climb. Lizzy was reluctant at first, but seeing she had no other options she slowly reached her hand forward.

I gripped her arm and we started our descent. My brain was clear and methodical, my grip strong. I managed to help Lizzy all the way down to the apron of shale rock, and knew she could handle it from there. I saw her mother running towards us. Lizzy reached her mom safely just as I was starting back up the cliff. There was no time to waste. I turned and headed for the next child, a young boy who looked to be no more than ten or eleven years old. He was directly above the spot where I had found Lizzy.

As I approached I heard a boy to my right yelling to me, "He's been hit bad. The rocks hit him real hard—I think he's hurt." I didn't know either one of these young boys, but at that instant I wanted to save them as badly as I would my own children.
I had to save them—failure wasn't an option. I reached the boy, grabbing his arm as I evaluated his condition. I could see several rocks had hit him. I was amazed he was still able to stand—no less than three softball-sized rocks had hit him in the head alone. As I made my way to him I could see the fear in his eyes, he was in a lot of pain and his head was bloody—I knew shock was imminent.

"Are you okay?" The boy shook his head and I could see he was crying.

He was mumbling incoherently—I couldn't understand what he was trying to say between his cries. "Calm down son, tell me again."

He calmed enough so I could understand what he was saying, "I had to stop them—I had to stop the rocks from hitting Lizzy."

I couldn't believe how heroic this eleven-year-old boy was—that he was brave enough to allow himself to be in the line of fire to save Lizzy.

"What's your name son?"

"Derrick."

"Okay Derrick, I'm going to hold onto your arm okay? I promise I won't let go, but you have to stay on your butt. Don't try and stand up. I'll help you down."

Derrick didn't appear to be able to respond, but signaled his agreement as he nodded his head. I held tight to his arms and we started another slow and treacherous descent. I repeated the same steps as I had with Lizzy, and we quickly reached the bottom. Kelsea was waiting with a small medical kit as I handed him off to her.

Two kids left and there wasn't much daylight. Every passing second was a second closer to either of the remaining boys losing their lives. I was only thinking of how to save them, completely forgetting any fears of my own. In the back of my mind I knew that one wrong step would spell disaster. I climbed on, coming in view of a young boy in a green shirt. He wasn't in the best physical shape. I started toward him, moving laterally up the side of the rock.

I heard his screams as I noticed the boy in the green shirt was slipping. He was frantically trying to get a hold with his feet but was unable to get any traction. He was sliding slowly towards the edge of the cliff. I took a quick look below and knew if he fell there was no chance that he would survive the fall.

I abandoned my careful movements up the side of the rock, my slow climb turning into a feverish sprint. I had no idea where the energy came from, but I kept climbing faster than I ever imagined I could. Just as I reached the boy, he slid forward as he lost his balance and was pitched towards the edge of the cliff. I reached out, catching him squarely across his chest. I pressed as hard as I could, pinning him to the side of the rock.

"I've got you," I told him as reassuringly as possible. My heart was racing and my brain felt like it was going to explode, but I tried to remain calm. Panic wasn't going to save his life, and could very well end up costing both of us dearly.

My brain cleared as another problem became evident. How was I going to get this kid down? I had come up the side so fast I couldn't remember which path I'd taken.

I managed to shift my grip to his arm, hanging onto him as I blindly lowered us down. My hands and feet felt like they were being placed by an unseen force or power. I had no idea what it was, but I was grateful for the help—at least, I knew I couldn't possibly be doing this on my own. As I carefully lowered us to safety, I dropped the boy off at the apron of loose rock and watched him walk off before starting back up again.

There was one child remaining to rescue, but my energy felt completely zapped. I looked to see the father of the last boy making his way up the slope toward his son. I felt more at ease to have some help, however, it quickly became obvious that this guy was anything but comfortable on the rock. I moved in their direction and noticed this was the boy had been hit by a large boulder I'd seen knocked loose by the father who had already made his way back to the top of the slope with his son. I assumed those two had escaped to safety and I didn't want to hamper the efforts of this father to save his son, but his awkward movements made me increasingly nervous.

He tried to tell his son where to step and move his feet, but was barely able to keep himself balanced in his own position.

"Don't tell him to move. He'll knock rocks down on us," I warned the father sternly.

"I can't get to him—I can't get to my son," he yelled back to me his voice filled with panic. I recognized him but didn't remember his name. Introductions at this point made no sense anyway—I didn't know why but I felt uncomfortable saving his boy without his permission.

It didn't make sense for both of us to place our lives in danger. I was close enough to see the boy's face was very pale, he wasn't going to be able to hold on much longer and his father seemed to notice it too.

"Can you save him? Will you save my son?" he pleaded with me. In an instant my brain processed what needed to be done—this father was placing his responsibility as his child's protector in my hands. The magnitude of that responsibility weighed on me, but I knew without question that I could do it.

I scooted up to the boy. He was lethargic and I was shocked he had held on for as long as he had. By now, he'd been in the same awkward position for at least twenty-five minutes. His back was bloodied and bulging from being blasted by the boulder. I had to get him down in a hurry. I reached up and grabbed his arm while I gave him the same speech I'd given the others.

We started our descent and within minutes arrived safely to the rock apron at the bottom. I held him by the arm until we reached the base of the apron. As I led him down, his father gathered him up, hugging him tightly as tears streamed down his face. He pulled away and looked back at me. Neither one of us said a word and nor did we need too. We both knew the situation—we both knew precious young lives were almost tragically lost.

His face said it all as he shook my hand with a strong firm grip before he turned and walked back to camp with his arm around his son's shoulders.

I turned to look at Kelsea. "I can't believe you saved them all!" she exclaimed, as I collapsed to my knees. It was like the energy switch that had been turned on for the last thirty minutes was suddenly and without warning turned off. I was overcome by emotions, my brain finally realizing the extent of what had happened. Kelsea knelt beside me and embraced me with a look in her eyes I will remember for the rest of my life. Lizzy's mom rushed up, thanking me profusely for what I had done. I didn't need the thanks—I just hoped someone would have done the same for my girls if they were the ones stuck on the cliff.

"They didn't even know!" Kelsea muttered. I couldn't understand what Kelsea was trying to say. "They all just continued on in the camp as if nothing was wrong."

I looked around and Kelsea was right. People were going about their activities, completely oblivious what had just happened just a few feet away.

"The boy in the green shirt walked over to his dad who just patted him on the head. He had no idea his son was within inches of losing his life."

I couldn't help but think that too many times there are dangers that not only inflict physical harm to our children, but mental and spiritual harm as well lurking all around us. How often had I noticed them? I thought of the mountain lion and what Gage had told me. Unless we know what to look for, danger is likely to creep up unnoticed. When we finally see it for what it is, it might be too late. In that moment, Gage's lesson took on even more meaning.

"How did you find the kids? I mean what made you notice they were in danger?" Kelsea asked.

"I heard their cries."

"Why didn't anyone else hear them?"

"I don't know. Maybe it's because I was in tune with my surroundings. I've spent the week with Gage and it's given me a new way to think about things. That might've had something to do with it, I guess."

"I'm glad you were in tune. I think we would have had a death here today if you hadn't heard the cry for help," Kelsea said.

"I know we would have!" I answered.

Truth be told, it didn't matter to me if I received any thanks from anyone. What mattered is that I was there and I had heard their cries for help. For whatever reason, I was in tune with my surroundings. I heard their voices over all the noise. A few people had gathered at the base of the cliffs, but for the most part no one had even heard me yell at the kids to stop. Right or wrong, everyone went about their activities without paying attention to their surroundings.

I wondered how many times I had allowed that to happen in my own life. Those times I didn't pay much attention to what was taking place around me—ignoring things almost on purpose. Those were the very things that could threaten to destroy me in one way or another. Is that why I lost my job? Did I not pay attention to the board when they made comments about plummeting stocks or mistakes that had cost the company millions? I'd felt impenetrable. I was successful, but I wasn't viewed that way. To the corporation,

I was a highly paid employee who meant nothing—someone else could easily continue my hard work, picking up right where I'd left off. Will they care about the Partition Project as much as I did? Probably not, but it doesn't matter. I should've seen it coming—I let my guard down because I'd failed to pay attention.

I was grateful I'd heard the children's cries for help. I wondered how many people around us are crying out for help but we ignore the signs? I took massive action to save those kids, but how many times do I spring into action to pull someone out of difficult situation they're struggling with? The cry is there—but do I listen? How do I feel this moment? Even though I saved those kids, I was completely exhausted.

My thoughts rested with the father trying to save his son. He didn't allow his ego to get in the way when it was evident he couldn't do it. He knew he had to rely on someone else, and he allowed that to happen. I'll remember his plea, "Please save my son!" for the rest of my life. The desperate look on his face as he pleaded for my help is imprinted on my soul. If he had not allowed me to help, the outcome would have been tragic.

Do I check my ego at the door? Do I allow the help of others no matter how good I think I am? Have I surrounded myself with people in my life who are willing and able to jump in and hear my cries? It goes both ways. And what about my little hero? Derrick placed himself in danger without hesitation. He wasn't going to allow any harm to come to Lizzy.
That boy already understands a perfect love for his fellow man—or at least for a little girl named Lizzy who wasn't going to get hurt on his watch.

I spent the remainder of the evening lying on my back looking up into the vast expanse of space as the stars flickered in the night sky. My life had changed for the better this week, but no day more so than today. I hadn't realized what I was capable of or how I would react to a situation like this until it happened. I was glad I had the opportunity to train this week with a master teacher like Gage. I was lost in my thoughts and didn't even notice Kelsea walk up and sit down next to me. The girls must have been fast asleep in their sleeping bags. I looked at Kelsea with the moonlight glowing on her face.

"Chance, I am so proud of you. You didn't hesitate—you sprang into action and directed a rescue operation that would normally take hours to plan. You're my hero."

As Kelsea spoke, I realized it didn't matter what happened with my interview at Kempton Motors. Nothing would be able to replace the way I felt at that moment. The lessons I had learned from Gage had just been put into practice, and not in a business setting as I'd thought they would. No, something much more important happened today. Now I knew that all I had to do was pay attention and look for opportunities. It no longer mattered if Donald gave me the job or not. I knew I'd figure something out. What mattered most to me is the way in which I choose to interact with others. Therein lies true success—the money will surely follow.

Author's Note

There are stories all around us that teach. All we have to do is find the lessons in each one.

Many of the stories told in Elephant Rock are true, although to my knowledge, no one has consulted with a ghost (at least no one will admit it). I've even known hunters who have encountered mountain lions on the Wasatch Mountain range of Utah. Their descriptions of these huge animals helped me write the scene where the mountain lion hunts Chance. My sisters and I really did sell multiple homemade items to earn a trampoline—one of the great lessons I learned from my dad.

The story about the grandmother who made all the blankets comes from a recollection of my own grandma, who passed away in February of 2012 at the age of 96. She made blankets for expectant mothers in need, up until about a year before her death when her eyesight gave out on her and she was simply unable to do it anymore. Her blankets have been shipped all over the world.

The epilogue is a true story that happened to a good friend of mine, an experienced hunter and tracker who has spent the majority of his life in the mountains.

On a family campout, he heard cries for help and sprang into action. His instincts saved the lives of those children that day and the experience changed his life forever. He shared his story with me at a perfect time, because it encompassed all of the lessons that Elephant Rock hopes to teach.

Made in the USA
Coppell, TX
15 September 2021

62427746R10075